THE BOSTON CELTICS
ALL-TIME ALL-STARS

THE BOSTON CELTICS ALL-TIME ALL-STARS

THE BEST PLAYERS AT EACH POSITION
FOR THE C'S

JOHN KARALIS

LYONS
PRESS

Guilford, Connecticut

An imprint of The Rowman & Littlefield Publishing Group, Inc.
4501 Forbes Blvd., Ste. 200
Lanham, MD 20706
www.rowman.com

Distributed by NATIONAL BOOK NETWORK

British Library Cataloguing in Publication Information available

Library of Congress Cataloging-in-Publication Data

Names: Karalis, John, author.
Title: The Boston Celtics all-time all-stars : the best players at each position for the Cs / John Karalis.
Description: Guilford, Connecticut : Lyons Press, 2020. | Includes bibliographical references. | Summary: "Combining statistical analysis, common sense, and a host of intangibles, long-time Celtics writer John Karalis constructs an all-time All-Star Boston Celtics line-up for the ages. Agree with his choices or not, you'll learn all there is to know about the men who played for and coached the most successful franchise in NBA history"— Provided by publisher.
Identifiers: LCCN 2020033342 (print) | LCCN 2020033343 (ebook) | ISBN 9781493046607 (paper) | ISBN 9781493046614 (epub)
Subjects: LCSH: Boston Celtics (Basketball team)—History. | Basketball—Massachusetts—Boston—History.
Classification: LCC GV885.52.B67 K37 2020 (print) | LCC GV885.52.B67 (ebook) | DDC 796.323/640974461—dc23
LC record available at https://lccn.loc.gov/2020033342
LC ebook record available at https://lccn.loc.gov/2020033343

CONTENTS

INTRODUCTION

Sports is an amazing diversion from the grind of day-to-day life. We pack stadiums to watch super-humans compete and do things we can never dream of doing ourselves. They are graceful and powerful, intelligent and cunning. On a basketball court, they combine in choreographed brilliance to execute complex game plans, somehow tossing a little ball through the air with amazing accuracy as other large humans try equally as hard to prevent it.

This is why it's funny to see a dude double-fisting Bud Light tallboys yelling at them about what they're doing wrong and how they should be playing the game.

But that's what sports is, and part of why it's beautiful. Because Joe 12-Pack can do that at a game. Because two seemingly reasonable and intelligent people can watch 48 minutes of the exact same game and have two completely different reactions to it.

This fuels an entire industry of talking heads, writers, bloggers, podcasters, networks, and so on. I'm lucky enough to be part of that machine, and, along with thousands of others, make a living off a game.

By sheer happenstance, my path crossed with one of the greatest franchises in all of organized sports. When my parents emigrated to the United States from Greece, they could have gone to any of the major Greek communities in the country. Lucky for me, they basically stopped once they hit land. If the Pilgrims landed on Plymouth Rock, my family was there to open up a pizza joint.

I didn't have the same experience as some of you. I don't have memories of going to the Boston Garden as a kid. I don't have those hazy memories of that rickety Green Line train stopping at North Station. I couldn't tell you how the arena felt, how the smell of stale cigarettes and cigar smoke became pleasant because they reminded me of when Dave Cowens did something awesome. I don't have that tear that forms in the corner of my eye when I see the parquet because Dad used to point out the dead spots to me.

I had to figure the Boston Celtics out all on my own. As I grew from a chubby young brillo-haired kid into a taller and taller teen, I was pushed into basketball. The better I got at the game, the more I wanted to consume it.

I started in the '80s, with Larry Bird, Kevin McHale, and Robert Parish. When I first started watching the Celtics play, before I was even a teenager, all I noticed was the ball going in. I was confused about how teams would win because it seemed like everyone was making all their shots. I didn't know anything about Indiana State's battle with Michigan State in 1979. I didn't know who Red Auerbach was or that he had recently ripped off the Golden State Warriors to make this team possible. The term *up and under* felt more like something Mom would tell me when it was time for bed.

As I got older, I started to realize what I'd stumbled onto. I got better at basketball, which made me want to watch more of it, and watching more of the Celtics made me better at basketball. I copied Kevin McHale's moves as often as I could, and wouldn't you know, they worked pretty well for me, too.

So I kept watching, and learning, and digging.

As the Celtics progressed past the Big 3, I'd spend time in libraries pulling out old encyclopedias to learn about the franchise (ahh, life before the internet). With each passing event in Celtics history, I tried to learn a little bit more about its past.

It's been a long time since my basketball Big Bang. The overarching lesson for me is simply that I'm lucky. We're lucky. Boston is lucky.

Professional sports matches are waged around the world on a daily basis, and they have for generations. Cities build identities around their home franchises. We live and die with their successes or failures. Winning fosters civic pride.

My entire basketball life, I've watched a team whose home is on the north side of Boston. Their wins gave me joy. Their losses gave me grief. I've cried tears of joy, anger, and sorrow because of them. Chances are you have too.

This is how sports works. Hundreds of men have pulled that green and white jersey over their heads. Hundreds of players have stuffed themselves into cramped locker rooms and inhaled Red's second-hand smoke in an effort to make us feel these feelings. Yet we have cheered for one team.

It's sort of like standing at a car wash all day and watching car after car after car roll by. You lose count after a while, but you've been in one place watching it all the whole time.

But what we've watched has been more amazing than anything any other basketball team has done: better than the Lakers, who started in Minnesota; better than the Knicks, who haven't exactly been very successful in their time in the so-called mecca of basketball (which is surprising for a city that has produced so many greats); better than Chicago, who might boast the greatest player of all time, but still not the greatest winner.

The hundreds of players who have passed through Boston include some of the best to ever pass through the National Basketball Association. When a team wins 17 championships, more than any other in league history, it goes without saying that some amazing players have played their part. All these outstanding players and teams make this book an interesting project, because Celtics history can be packaged in any number of ways.

We can create a team simply of the greatest winners of all time, a multiple-champions-only list of players to take on the basketball world. We can create a team built to win a championship in any era, pulling a 15-man roster together that can challenge any champion in any era and win. We can go decade-by-decade and build a super-team with just one from each year of the team's existence.

I could keep going with all sorts of examples, and each one could pull in a different group of players. The list of not only the greats, but guys who were elite at specific skills, is extensive. There are dozens of players from every era who deserve recognition.

For this exercise, though, we're going to limit it to just one dozen: 12 of the best who gave Boston their best and reached unbelievable heights, thrilling Boston fans by winning titles and making plays that didn't seem possible.

I wasn't lying when I said Boston was lucky. Some of the players on the list you're about to read would make any all-time team anywhere. Some would make the NBA's all-time team (and have through various specially marked league occasions). As I explore the breadth of their accomplishments, the depth of their desire to win, and the reverence they earned from teammates, you'll see why these guys became obvious choices.

I also had to make some hard choices to eliminate certain great players because they simply weren't great enough. This involved some inherently difficult cross-generational debates. How in the world can anyone properly compare Bill Sharman to Dennis Johnson?

There is some art to this: Subjectiveness in these debates is inherent, and you may certainly disagree with some of the choices. I surprised myself as some of my preconceived notions were wiped away the more I dug into players' pasts and, as best I could, some advanced analytics that leveled out differences in eras.

The result is a 12-man All-Time All-Star team. I discuss the top candidates for each position and whittle them down to two. At the end of each chapter, I name a starter and a reserve, creating a 10-man roster with two point guards, two shooting guards, two small forwards, two power forwards, and two centers. After that, I throw everyone who was eliminated back into the debate so I can pull out two wild cards from the mix to finish off the team.

Of course, no team is complete without a coach. My arbitrary cut-off line is 300 wins, so all Celtics head coaches to make that cut will be considered. From there, I'll choose a head coach and an assistant, pulling two from the pool just like I did with each position.

I'm pretty sure you can guess who the head coach will be. The rest makes for an interesting debate, as does the process of choosing the entirety of this team. It was a fun project for me to put together, and I hope it's a fun thing for you to read.

To me, this is more than just fodder for barroom banter. This is more than something a few people can debate on a podcast. Hopefully, you'll learn a little more about these guys and what made them so great. The goal here is not only to have fun with Celtics history, but to show you a little more of it, and maybe a side of some of it you didn't realize.

By the end, even if you agree with all of the selections, I hope you come away from this book with a deeper appreciation of the amazing history of the Boston Celtics and its collection of some of the greatest players of all time. I hope you put this book down and tell yourself, "wow, I'm lucky to love this franchise."

Here now is the Boston Celtics All-Time All-Star team.

POINT GUARD

The Candidates

Bob Cousy
K. C. Jones
Nate "Tiny" Archibald
Dennis Johnson
Rajon Rondo
Isaiah Thomas
Jo Jo White

A point guard is like the quarterback in football or a starting pitcher in baseball. They always have the ball in their hands, which means they get to control the game, determining the pace, the tempo, and the overall style of play.

All point guards have to dribble the ball, but they don't all have to be fancy. However, fancy dribblers had better be functional or else they'll be in a bit of trouble. The same applies to their passing.

Point guards need to be everyone's friend. They need to make sure the players who can score get the ball. They also have to be able to score a few points themselves. No position is more important to a team's offense, and the best of the best can increase their teammates' ability to score.

Bob Cousy

The Boston Celtics did not want Bob Cousy. Had they, he would have been the NBA's first ever draft pick. That distinction goes to Chuck Share, whom the Celtics chose with the top overall pick that year.

You see, the Basketball Association of America (BAA) and the National Basketball League (NBL) merged in 1949 and the new league was named the National Basketball Association. The NBA traces its history back to the BAA days, but the first NBA Draft was in 1950.

Anyway, Cousy was hooping it up up the Massachusetts Turnpike at Holy Cross in Worcester, scoring 1,775 points over the course of his career. He was a three-time All-American and, as his career might indicate, a magician with the basketball at a time when his flair was frowned upon.

Auerbach didn't care for it. He was a notorious hard-ass who wanted everything to be done a certain way. His way. The "right" way.

So when the Celtics had the first pick in the 1950 NBA Draft, they went with Share, a 6'11" center, instead of Cousy, the guy everyone wanted.

"I don't give a damn for sentiment," Red Auerbach, then the newly hired Celtics coach said. "The only thing that counts to me is ability and Cousy hasn't proven that he's got that ability. I'm not interested in bringing someone in just because he's a local yokel."

The pained look on the face of New York's Bob McNeill is indicative of how players felt trying to keep up with Cousy's on-court wizardry. (*NEW YORK WORLD-TELEGRAM AND THE SUN* VIA WIKIMEDIA COMMONS)

Side note: If you're a believer in destiny or things happening for certain reasons, then you need to keep this Cousy story handy. He essentially became that piece of cellophane wrapping that keeps sticking to your hands no matter how hard you try to get rid of it.

Cousy was drafted by the Tri-Cities Blackhawks, an early iteration of the Atlanta Hawks that, at the time, called Moline,

Illinois, home. Cousy didn't want to go to Moline because he was establishing a driving school in Worcester.

"That summer we had three cars going around the clock, and I wasn't giving a pro basketball career much thought," Cousy once said. "Then somebody calls me and says, 'Congratulations, you're the number one pick of the Tri-Cities Blackhawks.' My response was something like . . . 'What the hell is a Tri-Cities Blackhawk?'"

You have to remember that professional basketball in 1950 wasn't all about big contracts and sneaker deals. The sixth overall pick, Irwin Dambrot of City College of New York, decided not to play basketball and chose a career as a dentist instead. Cousy demanded a $10,000 salary from the Blackhawks to essentially cover what he would have made with his driving school. They refused.

So he was traded to the Chicago Stags instead, but they folded. Cousy and other Stags teammates were made available in a dispersal draft, which was conducted by lottery. The New York Knicks drew first and picked Max Zaslofsky, who had been a four-year, first-team All-BAA/All-NBA selection. The Celtics went second and team owner Walter Brown got Cousy.

It's important to know this whole story because it is the first brick in what is often a lucky foundation. Auerbach and the Celtics are known for slick moves and fleecing teams, but they might never have gotten the chance to pull the heists they did without a Zeus-level intervention by the Basketball Gods.

The next step if Boston had selected Zaslofsky was the heavens opening up with beams of sunlight blinding Brown and Auerbach and a booming voice declaring "YOU WILL

TAKE BOB COUSY NOW!" Even then Auerbach might have considered atheism over the flashy point guard.

Cousy took $9,000 from the Celtics and immediately became an All-Star in Boston, something he did 13 times in his career. He was a 10-time first-team All-NBA player and two-time second-teamer. He won the MVP in 1957, and the All-Star Game MVP (back when that was something that really mattered) twice. He was the first NBA player to get a *Sports Illustrated* cover, which also meant much more then than it does now.

Cousy won six championships in Boston, and was there for the beginning of Boston's magical 1960s run of eight straight.

He didn't shoot particularly well from the field, but then again no one did back then. In 1954, his 38.5 percent from the field was still good for 15th in the league. Teammates Ed Macauley and Bill Sharman were the only two players in the league to shoot better than 45 percent. Only 12 players shot at least 40 percent. But that didn't mean he couldn't shoot; it's just the style of play back then was super-fast and few guys had perfected the jump shot.

Again, the league was in its infancy. When the running and gunning stopped, Cousy was an 80 percent free throw shooter.

None of that really mattered when it came to Cousy, though. The scoring was secondary to his passing, and he led the league in assists for eight straight years. When he averaged a career-high 9.5 assists per game in 1960, it was 2.4 assists better than second-place Guy Rodgers.

It's also very important to note that assists in the 1950s and '60s were not handed out nearly as liberally as they are nowadays. In Cousy's day, the pass had to lead directly to a basket.

If a player dribbled before shooting, players would usually not get the assist, so there's no doubt that Cousy's numbers would be significantly better in today's NBA where players sometimes get two dribbles on assisted baskets.

The biggest thing Cousy is known for is his showmanship, fancy dribbling, and sometimes similarly fancy passes. Auerbach detested the flash, but the fast-breaking Celtics and Cousy were a perfect marriage. The style was sometimes just for fun, but it often had substance behind it. If it wasn't for Auerbach and Cousy reaching an agreement, that might not have been the case.

On the first day of practice, according to Auerbach, Cousy was throwing the ball all over the place. Already weary that Cousy had been getting the lion's share of the publicity, and afraid that Cousy would only get more flamboyant with his passing, Auerbach decided he needed to get a message across.

Auerbach said to him, "Bob, would you agree with me that guys like [Ed] Macauley and [Chuck] Cooper are pretty good athletes with quick hands?"

"Sure."

"Well, then, will you please tell me why they can't catch their passes? How come they're hitting these guys in the head, or bouncing off their chests, or just missing their fingertips?"

That proved to be a come-to-Jesus moment for Cousy. Red knew Cousy could have continued doing things his own way with the full support of Boston fans and media. Red knew he was taking a risk that could have made this job just as unbearable as the jobs he'd quit before taking this one. If Cousy chose to be petulant and arrogant, he could have told Auerbach off and made things difficult for everyone.

"But he didn't," Auerbach said. "He looked at me and said, 'What am I doing wrong?' Right then I knew I had a superstar on my hands."

Whether he was drawing defenders, dribbling out a clock, or trying to get himself some space to drive, the famous Cousy ball-handling and passing skills that earned him the nickname "Houdini of the Hardwood" were often as much function as flair.

Here's another generational element to Cousy's game that should be highlighted: Players were not allowed to put their hands on the side of the ball when they dribbled.

Cousy detractors will have some fun mixing his high-lights with the famous clip of Stanley playing basketball on *The Office*. Without the proper context, it's easy to say he didn't look particularly smooth compared to today's ball-handling wizards.

However, if Kyrie Irving were to step through a wormhole into 1960, he'd turn the ball over every time he tried to cross someone over. Every time he hesitated on a dribble or put his hand on the side of the ball to control it better, he'd be called for a palming violation. That's just how it was back then.

Cousy became the NBA's first true star player. People were dazzled by something they just hadn't seen on the floor until he showed up.

"Cousy had a great intellect," said former teammate K. C. Jones. "He quickly became famous for those behind-the-back passes and the fancy dribbling. Red called the fancy stuff 'French pastries,' but Cousy was very successful with it. He always had a high number of assists, and he had that on-the-run, one-foot shot. That was one of his trademarks."

Of course, had the league been more integrated during his time, maybe Cousy's career would have been different. However, we have what we have as far as NBA history, and I have all the confidence in the world a player as good as Cousy could have figured out a way to stand out no matter what. You can tell by how other stars talked about him, even when they only had a short time with him on the floor.

"Cousy always had the presence of mind to find me in situations where I was able to move and free myself for an open shot," John Havlicek, who played one year with Cousy, said. "His court vision was unbelievable, and it helped me to see the court better—the passing lanes, the angles, things like that."

There are other very good players on this list, but there is simply no point guard in Boston Celtics history that can supplant him as the best. The innovation on the court, the vision and ability to make his teammates better, and his overall impact as one of the league's foundational players make this too easy of a call to make.

Bob Cousy is not only on Boston's All-Time All-Star team, he's easily the starting point guard.

Who backs him up?

That's not so easy.

K. C. JONES

K. C. Jones, a teammate of Cousy's for six years, needs to be mentioned simply because he was, perhaps, as close to an equal defensively to Bill Russell as anyone was at the time.

Jones was Russell's college teammate at San Francisco, but he took a detour to actually revolutionize defense in another sport.

There's a very good chance this K. C. Jones layup came off one of his own steals. He was perhaps the most fearsome perimeter defender of his time. Having him and Bill Russell on the same team really wasn't fair to opposing offenses. (WIKIMEDIA COMMONS)

Jones spent some time as a defensive back for the Los Angeles Rams. He used his strength and speed to line up close to receivers, hit them, and then keep stride with them as they ran off into their routes.

It eventually became known as "bump and run" coverage. If things had gone differently, Jones might have been a solid choice in a Rams All-Time All-Stars book. Instead, he hurt his knee and gave Red Auerbach a call to see if a spot for him still existed on the team that had drafted him in the second round of the 1956 draft.

He joined the team in 1958 and was on every one of Boston's eight straight championship teams. He did a very nice job controlling the game offensively while being a maniacal defender. He was, in essence, Marcus Smart before Marcus Smart existed. He was very necessary to every one of those championships, so much so that his number was retired and he earned induction into the Hall of Fame while averaging just 7.4 points and 3.5 rebounds per game.

Jones took over for Cousy when he retired.

"The fans responded by not coming to the games in the same numbers," Jones said, understanding that Cousy was a box office draw. But he also felt that he had what it took to be a starter. "I was very confident in my abilities as a defender. If you were a master of defense, then I was convinced that you could match the offensive player at any level. And the fear factor disappeared."

Jones was never an offensive player. There's no chance of him earning a backup spot on this team, but he was so good in so many other ways that it would have been criminal to not mention him and why he was so important to the team's success. He's one of the best defenders the league has ever seen. It's why he's in the Hall of Fame with career scoring averages of 7.4 points, 3.5 rebounds, and 4.3 assists per game.

Jones wasn't just some tagalong for eight championships. Boston was a fast-breaking team that ran opponents out of the gym. They needed defenders to turn people over and get running the other way. If Bill Russell wasn't blocking them at the rim, Jones was ripping it from them. I'd love to tell you how many times he did that, but they didn't track steals back then.

So many other guys get so much credit for that monster run in the '60s. It's time Jones got his shout-out for his role, too.

Now that that's out there, let's dive into the meat of this backup debate. Here's how the rest of the candidates stack up statistically:

Archibald

5 seasons, 12.5 ppg, 46.9% FG, 7.1 apg, 1.9 rpg, 3 All-Star appearances, 1 championship, 1 All-NBA

Johnson

7 seasons, 12.6 ppg, 44.6% FG, 6.4 apg, 3.2 rpg, 1 All-Star appearance, 2 championships, 5 All-Defense

Rondo

9 seasons, 11 ppg, 47.3% FG, 8.5 apg, 4.7 rpg, 4 All-Star appearances, 1 championship, 1 All-Rookie, 4 All-Defense, 1 All-NBA

Thomas

3 seasons, 24.7 ppg, 44.3% FG (36.8% 3 pt), 6 apg, 2.7 rpg, 2 All-Star appearances, 1 All-NBA

White

10 seasons, 18.4 ppg, 44.2% FG, 5.1 apg, 4.3 rpg, 7 All-Star appearances, 2 championships, 1 All-Rookie, 2 All-NBA, 1 Finals MVP

NATE "TINY" ARCHIBALD

Archibald's career changed when he tore his Achilles tendon as a Buffalo Brave in 1977. Before the injury, he was a flashy scorer who, until recently, was the only player to lead the NBA in points and assists in a single season. The 6'1" Archibald challenged everyone on the floor and often won.

With the Cincinnati Royals, Kansas City Kings, and New York Nets, he was a 25-point-per-game, All-NBA kind of scorer. (He never played a regular-season game for the Braves.)

That's not who he was as a Celtic.

The post-injury Archibald showed up in Boston in 1978 out of shape and out of sorts.

"I weighed 240 pounds when I got to Boston," said Archibald, who spent most of his playing days at about 170 pounds. "Red took one look at me and said that if I didn't lose the weight that I wouldn't play. It wasn't that he didn't want me, because he did. He just didn't want two of me!"

After a disaster of a first season with the Celtics, Archibald adjusted his game. The score-first, attacking Archibald took a

Tiny Archibald never even averaged half of what he did at his best in Kansas City, but half his career All-Star appearances came as a Boston Celtic. (STEVE LIPOFSKY WWW.BASKETBALLPHOTO.COM)

back seat to Larry Bird and Cedric Maxwell, letting them handle the heavy scoring burden while he ran the offense.

"Red Auerbach needed a quarterback to run his team, especially since he was assembling such a talented front line," Archibald said. "By that time in my career I was more than ready to share the load offensively. I'd been a big-time scorer, but I hadn't gone deep in the playoffs. I wanted a ring."

It was exactly what the Celtics needed. Archibald's guidance was key to Boston's 1981 championship. He'd score when he had to, topping 20 points in four of Boston's playoff wins that year. Mostly he was a supporting scorer who averaged more than 15 points and six assists per game in the championship run.

Archibald had an amazing career. He's a Hall of Famer. For the purposes of this discussion, he just didn't do enough as a Celtic to supplant any of the competition.

DENNIS JOHNSON

Johnson had some parallels with Archibald. Both had reputations for having less-than-ideal attitudes prior to joining the Celtics, but both had plenty of success and had to adjust their games with their new team.

It was Johnson's reputation as a hothead that got him to Boston in the first place. He made the All-Star team four times before joining Boston, twice as a member of the Seattle Supersonics and twice as a Phoenix Sun. He was a second-team All-NBA player and Finals MVP in 1979, and yet Seattle still traded him away in his prime.

Two of his most productive years of his career were spent in Phoenix, and he made his only first-team All-NBA as a Sun, yet they basically gave him to Boston in 1983.

Johnson was the glue that kept the Big 3 together and was one of the best shot-blocking guards of all time. He blocked three shots in a game seven separate times over his career. (STEVE LIPOFSKY WWW.BASKETBALL PHOTO.COM)

Boston sent Phoenix Rick Robey, a career backup center, and two second rounders for Johnson, a first round pick, and a third round pick. If you don't know who Rick Robey is, don't worry. You shouldn't.

Johnson also saw the move to Boston as more exposure for him after playing in relative obscurity in Seattle and Phoenix. There was no League Pass or internet back then, and major markets got all the exposure. A move to Boston was a chance to be seen.

"The so-called experts were saying that the Suns practically gave me away because I was a problem child," Johnson said. "That bothered me, but I used it as motivation. In the end, joining the Celtics was a dream come true, because I got to compete for championships with guys like Larry, Robert, and Kevin."

Even with bridges burned at his past stops, Johnson came to a team that welcomed him with open arms.

"Johnson fills one of our most important needs," Auerbach said at the time. "We got a strong defensive guard who also averaged 14.2 points a game last season. We now have a big guard who can play the big guards like Magic Johnson and Reggie Theus."

Defense was Johnson's hallmark. In DJ, Boston had the perfect point guard to pair with their Big 3 front line of Larry Bird, Kevin McHale, and Robert Parish. He'd score when needed, but mostly he'd initiate the Celtics offense and defend the opposing team's best perimeter player. In his day, guards could get physical, and Johnson took advantage. He was also one of the best shot-blocking guards the league has ever seen.

Bird often called Johnson the best teammate he ever had, which is an amazing sign of respect from a person like him. Bird admired hard work, professionalism, and on-court intelligence.

Johnson never tried to do too much (though he'd occasionally get criticized for doing too little in games of little consequence). He just got the ball moving, found Bird when he needed to, and played his role to the best of his abilities.

The highlight of their bond came in 1987, in the famous Bird steal against the Detroit Pistons.

If you remember Johnny Most's famous radio call, it came in two parts: the steal, and the finish.

"Annnnd *there's a steal by Bird! Underneath to DJ and he lays it in!*"

Bird's steal was iconic, but it would have meant nothing without Johnson's equally intelligent recognition of the play and the dive to the basket to get the pass from Bird, who was trying to keep his balance on the baseline.

"The steal doesn't matter if DJ doesn't have the presence of mind to cut to the basket," Bird said of the play. "We lose that game. Dennis always played better when the stakes were higher. I thought the world of Dennis Johnson."

Bird gets all the love for making the play, and deservedly so, but no one remembers that play if Johnson isn't in the perfect place at the perfect time to catch that pass and make that basket. After the play, the camera caught the perfect moment.

It was Larry Bird, waving Johnson over on his way to the bench, and giving him a hug.

Bird knew it too.

Is this enough to get DJ onto this team? He would certainly be its best perimeter defender by a mile. A basketball team with Johnson and Bill Russell (spoiler alert: Russell probably makes this team) would be among the most feared defensive teams of all time.

Rajon Rondo

Rajon Rondo, at least the Celtics version, would also have been a pretty good defender. Somewhere along the way, probably after his torn ACL, Rondo backed off his defensive effort. In many ways, Rondo was DJ 2.0, except with supercharged court vision.

Johnson was often considered a point guard in name only. It was, indeed, his position, but Larry Bird was the team's best passer and the offense ran through him. Rondo, though, was very clearly the best passer not only on the Celtics, but maybe in the entire league, at the height of his powers.

He was exactly what the new Big 3 needed in their late 2000s run. Paul Pierce, Ray Allen, and Kevin Garnett were in the sweet spots of their careers where they were still good enough to perform, but hungry enough for a title to sacrifice to make it work. All they needed was a point guard to make sure everybody was happy.

People like to use the word *savant* to describe the highly intelligent, but Rondo truly was. He had a next-level intelligence for the game that often led to clashes with his coach, another thing he had in common with Johnson.

"Rondo is and was smarter than most people in the room," said former teammate and current Celtics color analyst Brian Scalabrine. "I would say he's on the same level as Doc Rivers if you want to compare and Doc is an extremely intelligent guy."

Extremely intelligent might not even be enough to cover it.

"He knows everything. You think he just knows his position, sometimes, but no. He knows everybody's position," said former teammate Leon Powe. "But also, he knows the opposing team's positions as well, where they're supposed to be on

Rajon Rondo might have been the smartest man in the building whenever a game was played. That led to some clashes with teammates and coaches, including one where he threw a water bottle through a TV during a film session. He was fined $20,000 for that. (ERIC KILBY VIA WIKIMEDIA COMMONS)

the floor as well. In one game he told one player where to go on the floor. He wasn't on our team. He said 'excuse me, you're supposed to be in the left corner' and I looked up and was like, 'did he just say that to him?' And everybody started cracking up but that's Rondo. He knows everything."

The Rivers/Rondo dynamic was volatile, but it worked for the Celtics on the court. They won a championship in Rondo's second year. He dished out 12 or more assists four times in the Celtics playoff run, and dropped a 21-point, 8-assist, 7-rebound, 6-steal gem in the deciding Game 6 over the Los Angeles Lakers.

The longer the team played together, the more Rondo realized his full power. It turns out he was more Sith than Jedi, though, as the stronger he got, the more headstrong and volatile he became.

Rondo threw some of the most beautiful passes you'll ever see. On a random March day in Oakland, Rondo torched the Golden State Warriors with a spinning, behind-the-back pass to Allen who caught it in the corner, on the move, perfectly in his shooting pocket. It was something out of a Bugs Bunny cartoon where the slick shooter tossed a silver dollar in the air, shot it, and four quarters fell into his hand.

However, Rondo's intimate knowledge of opponents and their tendencies, along with his ability to make just about any pass he wanted, manifested itself in a bit of assist-hunting, which divided the fan base and started to rankle some inside the locker room. On one side, he had three straight seasons averaging more than 11 assists per game. A point guard is supposed to find his teammates for baskets, and he found them.

Still, he was accused of stalling the offense and reducing some teammates to standing and waiting until Rondo had deemed it their turn to score. To make matters worse, Rondo's inability to shoot was becoming an issue as the NBA started morphing into an analytics-driven league that realized how much more valuable the 3-point shot had become.

Rondo overcame that lack of shooting, in part, by channeling his stubbornness into an absolute refusal to give up regardless of injury. In 2011, Rondo was pulled down by Miami's Dwyane Wade, landing awkwardly on his arm and dislocating his left elbow. He came back with the arm heavily wrapped and finished the game. It was Boston's only win in the series. He tore his ACL in 2013, but played 12 minutes on it before he came out to get his knee checked.

Whether it was that injury or just a decision to conserve his energy, Rondo's defense tailed off dramatically after the 2011-12 season. By then Allen was long gone and Rivers was about to leave as well. Garnett and Pierce were traded in the summer of 2013 and Rondo was traded in 2014. Rondo's reputation had taken a dive, just like the Celtics record.

It's possible none of this would have mattered had injuries not robbed Boston of chances to win additional titles in 2009 and 2010. Rondo could have been a three-time champion in the first four years of his career. He could have cemented himself as a challenger to Cousy's brilliance, the modern day Houdini.

His style was certainly worthy. His stats keep him in the conversation as perhaps the Celtics' single-greatest assist-man when he was at his best (though there's a very easy argument to make that if they swapped places, Cousy's assist numbers would look more like Rondo's thanks to more liberal application of the assist rules). Was his run long enough and brilliant enough to back up Cousy on this team?

ISAIAH THOMAS

There is one fact to consider in this debate: Isaiah Thomas had the best single season of all the potential candidates.

Thomas's 2016-17 run with the Celtics was nothing short of magical.

"Ridiculous," Brad Stevens, who coached Thomas during his time as a Celtic said of his run that season. "That's what the title should be."

The biggest obstacle for Thomas in this debate, however, is the same one he faces as a player: It's too short.

The 5'9" Thomas was swept into Boston in Danny Ainge's whirlwind 2014-15 season. Two months after Rondo was sent away to Dallas, Thomas was acquired from the Phoenix Suns. It was one of 10 (10!) trades Ainge had executed between the end of the previous season and the trade deadline.

Thomas was an instant hit, mostly because of what would normally be an inauspicious beginning to one's career.

Thomas was ejected from his first game as a Celtic, but because it came against the Lakers in Los Angeles, fans loved him for it. He also carried a struggling team into the playoffs, leading Boston to a 20-10 record after taking the floor as a new Celtic. Boston was 20-32 without him that year.

"That team—we had our things that we weren't as good at, but we were really tough," Stevens said. "That toughness, he helped lead. Everybody knew he was going to compete, that he was always gonna be there at the end to make a play. He wore

Isaiah Thomas set records in 3-pointers made and attempted as a Celtic. He also set the unofficial record for "quickest to capture the fanbase's hearts." (STEVE LIPOFSKY WWW.BASKETBALLPHOTO.COM)

that chip on his shoulder and I think we all followed that chip on his shoulder."

They expectedly got swept by LeBron James and the Cleveland Cavaliers, but Thomas's reputation was cemented in Boston. He was instantly loved as a hard-working overachiever, and his following two seasons did nothing but cement that reputation.

Those were both All-Star seasons for Thomas, the only two of his career. He helped lead the Celtics to a 48-34 record in 2015-16, and a shocking 53-29 record and the number one seed in 2016-17.

Thomas averaged 28.9 points per game that year, one point shy of Larry Bird's team record for points per game in a single season. His 2,199 points are the fifth-most in a single season for a Celtic. His 52-point game against Miami on December 30, 2016, is the fourth-most points a Celtic has scored in a regular-season game, and the 53 he scored in Game 2 of the team's semifinal matchup against the Washington Wizards was one point short of John Havlicek's record.

Things like "best games" are subjective, partly because few of us have been alive long enough to remember all of the details, but it's hard to imagine a better, more meaningful game than that 53-point performance by Thomas.

Before those playoffs started Thomas learned that his 22-year-old sister had been killed in a car crash. He played every game, seven in all, prior to this game on May 2, 2017.

That was Chyna's birthday.

Thomas had already undergone surgery to repair a tooth that was broken the game before.

"It just wasn't a good day for me with it being my sister's birthday, me being in the hospital for three or four hours today," Thomas said. "I just didn't have the energy. But once I got around the guys, got to the arena, I felt like I could go. And I told [coach Brad Stevens] I could. There was no way I couldn't play on [Chyna's] birthday. I wanted to win for her. I wanted to play well for her."

Said Stevens, "I remember seeing him after it happened and telling him 'do what you need to do, don't play.' He said 'I gotta play. That's what I like to do and it's my sanctuary.' I remember him playing in the Chicago series, flying back, doing the funeral, coming back for Game 1. We're down 16-nothing, he helped will us to that one. He gets hit, two days later, on her birthday, with 10 hours of dental surgery, he has 53 points. Unreal. I mean, unreal."

Thomas willed the Celtics to victory in a game they had no business winning. It was par for the course that season, but it was his 29-point fourth quarter, especially under those circumstances, that etches the performance in Celtics lore. Thomas became a mythological figure that day, forever etched in the memories of a generation.

The final twist of Thomas's career was a tragedy of Shakespearian proportions. He suffered a hip injury against the Cleveland Cavaliers in the Eastern Conference Finals. It had been revealed that the injury was something ongoing, and Thomas had been trying to play through it. When he could no longer, the closer look revealed a degenerative condition that required surgery.

In the midst of his rehabilitation, he was traded to Cleveland for Kyrie Irving. The Boston hero was gone, unable to rekindle the magic elsewhere.

What were those three seasons worth? Is the most dominant performance of any candidate here enough to overcome the flash that was his Celtics career? Is one of the greatest offensive performances in NBA history enough to match longer, less singularly amazing runs?

Jo Jo White

If you could somehow mash up all these choices, the end result might be Jo Jo White. He had the longevity, the accolades, and the potency to challenge any of these other candidates.

His basketball ability spoke for itself, but beyond that he was known for two things: being able to play forever and being one of the sharpest dressers in the league.

Look, we're talking about an All-Star Game here. We want at least one of these guys to be someone Instagrammable in today's era, don't we?

Let's circle back on that and start with the important stuff first.

"Jo Jo White was one of the most clutch but underrated Celtics of all time," said Celtics historian and blogger for RedsArmy.com, Mike Dynon. "He was one of the NBA's top combo guards during an era when there was little distinction between point guard and shooting guard. Jo Jo was equally comfortable handling the middle of a fast break, directing a halfcourt offense, or curling off screens for a stop-and-pop with his deadly midrange jumper."

Jo Jo White was silky smooth on and off the court. White remains in the top 10 of many Celtics offensive lists, including points, field goals, and field goals attempted. (WIKIMEDIA COMMONS)

White joined the Celtics fresh off a stint with the United States Marine Corps, so he was uniquely prepared for the rigors of the NBA. He'd also been drafted by the Dallas Cowboys and Cincinnati Reds, so the Celtics knew they were also getting an amazing all-around athlete.

White played in 488 straight games for the Celtics, including five straight years of playing in all 82 games (and averaging nearly 40 minutes per game while doing so).

He joined a team coached by Tommy Heinsohn, who was raised on the Auerbach run-and-gun style of basketball. He wanted guys who would push the ball, and White was more than happy to do that, even though he hadn't been an up-tempo guy in college.

His rookie year was a tough one. Boston finished 34-48 in the first season of the post–Bill Russell/Sam Jones era. His next year was the first of seven All-Star seasons for White (whose real name is Joseph, but he earned the nickname "Jo Jo" because coaches would have to yell his name twice to get his attention as a younger player). His second season was also the last time he'd miss a game until 1978.

Through the course of those years, he not only led the Celtics to two titles, he engaged in a rivalry with the hated New York Knicks and their own star point guard, Walt "Clyde" Frazier. They both had seven All-Star seasons, six of which overlapped.

"During much of his career, Jo Jo was compared to Frazier, who got more hype because he played in New York. But I always felt that Jo Jo was Clyde's equal in every way on the court," Dynon said. "In the end, they both owned two rings and both made it to the Hall of Fame—but only Jo Jo was a Finals MVP."

White quietly went about his business, though, averaging 18.4 points per game in his 10 years as a Celtic. Unlike some of the other candidates on this list, the ultra-disciplined ex-Marine was a dream on and off the court. The loudest thing about him were his outfits.

And boy were they spectacular.

"With Jo Jo White, if you were a Celtic, that personified cool," his former teammate Cedric Maxwell told The Undefeated after White's passing from a brain tumor. "He did everything so cool. He walked cool. He talked cool. He was just the ultimate during the '70s. I would say he was, 'K-O-O-L, not 'C,' but 'K-O-O-L.'

"The first time I saw Jo Jo he was in a pinstriped blue suit, and 'Damn' was the only thing that came out of my mouth. And then to watch him play, he had gotten older and lost a step. But to watch him play, he had flashes where you can see that All-Star."

Side note: I once bumped into Jo Jo White waiting for a table in a restaurant in Cambridge and I can confirm these stories about his style and swagger.

White had the style and grace. He has the stats and rings. He has two All-NBA nods and an All-Rookie. He also has the signature moment.

"Most of all, Jo Jo is known for his clutch performance in Game 5 of the 1976 Finals, Boston's triple-overtime win over the Phoenix Suns that's widely considered the greatest game in NBA history," Dynon said. "With the series tied 2–2, Jo Jo played 60 of Game 5's 63 minutes, scored 33 points on 15-of-29 shooting, and added 9 assists and 6 rebounds. He hit a key free throw that prevented the Suns from winning in the second OT, and closed out the game by dodging defenders and dribbling out the clock to preserve a two-point lead. The Celtics won the series in six games and Jo Jo was named MVP. He deserved it."

"I personally would have to say it was one of the greatest games, and I was very happy to be a part of it," White would later say in an online chat with fans. "It was draining. It was strenuous. You had to reach down for everything you had to pull out a victory. It had all the dramatics that anyone could ask for.

"Fatigue became a factor. I was tired, but I was conditioned to go the distance, so my thinking was that if I was tired, the other players were close to death," he added. "So that gave me motivation to push on, and any athlete worth his salt would want to be on the floor for that game, and I was up to the task."

He was indeed, and the performance was part of what earned him the Finals MVP that year. While it was his most memorable moment, it wasn't his only one.

"There was another moment two years earlier that also demonstrated how clutch Jo Jo was," Dynon said. "The Celtics held a 3–2 lead in their first-round playoff series vs. the Buffalo Braves, and were on the road for Game 6. With the score tied, Jo Jo was fouled at the buzzer and went to the free throw line with a chance to end the series. He ignored the screaming crowd and swished both shots. The Celtics went on to win the 1974 NBA title."

The Celtics have had some amazing point guards over the years. Archibald changed his game and became an integral piece to a champion. Johnson did the same, and both have been underrated for years. Rondo was on a path to greatness in Boston but circumstances and bad luck derailed that, as it did with

Isaiah Thomas. And even though Thomas had one of the most brilliant seasons in team history, it's just not enough to supplant White.

The 1970s are a dark, complicated time in NBA history, and that's probably part of why the stars of that era are so underrated. The ABA arrived as a serious challenge to the NBA with its carefree style and innovations like the 3-point shot. It caused a bit of a racial divide, with the ABA's more playground-style of basketball attracting some of the game's more creative players while the NBA stuck to a more button-down approach.

The '70s also brought with it drug scandals, which further drove fans away, and by the end of it, there were serious questions about the league's viability. Stars like White missed out on their chance for proper due, and so they're often overlooked in debates like this.

Frankly, before I really dove into this chapter, I had already decided that Cousy and DJ were going to be my point guards, but White's career is just too good to overlook. I'm a child of the '80s, and I'll forever love Dennis Johnson for what he meant to the Big 3. He will forever be an underappreciated part of that era.

However, White is simply too good. If he was the main point guard in any different era, there's a strong chance he'd be better appreciated. The fluidity with which he played the game was mesmerizing. The stories of NBA ironmen begin with John Havlicek, but White was right there with him, step-for-step, logging minutes that would never be allowed in today's game.

White could handle all phases of the game and do it all smoothly. Then, after tearing a team apart, he'd walk out of the arena looking as sharp as the game he'd just played.

There is no doubt here that Jo Jo White is a part of Boston's All-Time All-Star team.

Final verdict:
Starter: Bob Cousy
Backup: Jo Jo White

SHOOTING GUARD

The Candidates
John Havlicek
Sam Jones
Bill Sharman
Reggie Lewis
Ray Allen
Danny Ainge

Shooting guard is a fun position in basketball because it's the only position where "shooting" is built into the job description. Everyone loves to shoot the ball. Shooting equals scoring and scoring equals fame and glory.

Plays are run for shooting guards. They're not asked to do much dribbling or passing, at least not as much as some others. Just catch the ball, and shoot it.

Pretty sweet gig if you ask me.

JOHN HAVLICEK
Go ahead, call me a cheater if you'd like, but Havlicek, still Boston's all-time leading scorer, was listed as both a shooting guard and small forward. In today's NBA, you could just call

Still photographs are the only time Havlicek was ever seen not moving.
(STEVE LIPOFSKY WWW.BASKETBALLPHOTO.COM [LEFT], THE *SPORTING NEWS* VIA
WIKIMEDIA COMMONS)

him a wing, but in this book, I'm calling him a shooting guard because it makes life easier on me and it helps keep a wild card slot open.

The real debate at the two-guard spot will be who makes it to the bench, because no one is making it past Havlicek. He scored more than 30,171 combined regular-season and playoff points without benefit of a 3-pointer. He "stole the ball." He's on the team.

Except, he almost wasn't.

Like most professional athletes, Havlicek was exceptional at most any athletic endeavor as a young man. The Martins Ferry, Ohio, native was an All-Stater in basketball, football, and baseball. While Havlicek was drafted by the Boston Celtics with the seventh pick in the 1962 draft, the Cleveland Browns also decided to take him with a late-round pick and give him a shot at wide receiver.

Havlicek gave it a go with the Browns, but was part of the team's final cuts, so he was off to Boston.

I don't know what the football equivalent to his NBA career would have been, but I'd imagine he would have been in the Cris Carter or Randy Moss stratosphere, except, you know, with a bunch of championships. He actually used those skills to his advantage.

"He didn't really shoot from the outside or dribble that much," Tommy Heinsohn, who was both a teammate and coach to Havlicek, once said. "But he was like a wide receiver in football, and he would run and catch long passes from Cousy for layups."

He won four straight titles to start his career and six in his first seven seasons. He'd tack on two more before retiring with

13 All-Star and All-NBA selections on his resume, as well as nine All-Defensive selections and a Finals MVP. Bill Russell called him "the best all-around player I ever saw."

If there's one immutable rule in life, it's that Bill Russell is never wrong about basketball. However, All-Stars are about numbers, and the numbers back him up.

Havlicek averaged 20.8 points per game over the course of his 16-year career, never averaging fewer than 14.3. He had an eight-year stretch of averaging 20-plus points per game, topping out at 28.9 in 1970-71. He was the first player to score 1,000 or more points in 16 consecutive seasons. He also averaged a career-high nine rebounds and 45.4 minutes per game.

Let's call a 20-second timeout to fully grasp the absurdity of this. There are 48 minutes in an NBA game. He spent the 1971 season resting for 2.4 minutes a game, over 81 games. The next year he played all 82 and averaged 45.1 minutes. He spent five straight years averaging more than 40.

We like to talk about unbreakable records and things of that nature a lot. It's hard to imagine, especially in today's era of "load management," that anyone would come close to 45 minutes a game anymore.

Hall of Famer Bailey Howell said Havlicek was one of the toughest matchups in the league.

"He was big enough to play forward and quick enough to play guard," he said. "Because of these advantages, he really presented problems wherever he was asked to play. He could run the floor against the big, slow guys, and he could step out on the quick guards and really play great defense."

So it should be no surprise that Hondo, as he was known because of a resemblance to John Wayne, remains the team's leader in not only points, but minutes and games played. He famously had a low heart rate and overly large lungs that allowed him to run, almost literally, all day long. He never seemed to be tired or out of breath, which is how he was able to stay on the court that long. It's what allowed him to become one of the league's best ever two-way players. It's why Russell used to crack that Havlicek was some kind of wind-up doll.

New York Knicks coach Red Holzman once said Havlicek's stamina alone would be enough to make him one of the best to ever play the game.

"It would've been fair to those who had to play him or those who had to coach against him if he had been blessed only with his inhuman endurance. God had to compound it by making him a good scorer, smart ballhandler and intelligent defensive player with quickness of mind, hands and feet."

Frankly, it's almost not fair to have that kind of stamina and be great at the sport. It's sort of like how it's not fair that Cristiano Ronaldo is one of the best soccer players ever and devastatingly handsome. You can have a very nice life being one or the other; being both just mocks us mere mortals.

For example, a 35-year-old Havlicek cranked his way through 58 minutes of an epic triple-overtime game in the 1976 NBA Finals. Considering he'd torn his left plantar fascia at the beginning of the playoffs, it's a wonder he was even playing, let alone leading the Celtics to a win in the greatest Finals game in NBA history.

Most people know him from the famous Johnny Most "Havlicek stole the ball" moment in 1965. After a Russell pass hit a guide wire on an inbounds play during Game 7 of the

Eastern Division Finals, Philadelphia was given the ball and a chance to inbound down 110–109.

Havlicek had Red Auerbach's voice in his head telling him to always figure out how to find an edge. So, knowing Hal Greer had five seconds to inbound the ball, he counted down the seconds in his head and then broke for the pass knowing it had to be thrown in.

"I could actually try to time the pass and have a shot at deflecting or stealing the inbounds pass," he said. "So I counted. One thousand one, one thousand two, one thousand three. . . ."

He broke on one thousand four, stole it, and got it to Sam Jones. Most's iconic call sealed that play in Celtics lore forever.

It's actually a bit odd that Havlicek is almost overlooked when discussing the Celtics greats. Given a choice between him and Larry Bird or him and Bill Russell, most people would take Bird or Russell. Tommy Heinsohn, himself a candidate for this All-Time All-Star team as both a player and coach, has called Paul Pierce, not Havlicek, the greatest scorer in team history.

Havlicek was everything that would make a Boston sports icon. He worked tirelessly, won championships, played through injury, and he did it all at a Hall of Fame level, mostly while coming off the bench.

Yeah, he was a sixth man.

Sorry, he was *the* sixth man.

"It never bothered me," he said, "because I think that role is very important to a club. One thing I learned from Red Auerbach was that it's not who starts the game, but who finishes it, and I generally was around at the finish."

Maybe it's just more fitting that his amazing career was a bit understated, because that's who Havlicek was. I'm not going to be understated though. Havlicek, who died in 2019, might make the NBA's All-Time All-Star team, not just Boston's. He was a selfless badass who ran forever, scored a ton, and defended like hell. There's no bench role for him on this team. He's a starter.

Now the question is, who backs him up?

BILL SHARMAN VS. SAM JONES

There is a lot of firepower from which to choose. Let's start with the contemporaries, Sharman and Jones. Bob Cousy played with both, so he'd know better than anyone which guy to choose.

"The way I looked at it, Sam and Bill Sharman are probably most responsible for me getting into the Hall of Fame," Cousy said. "Because whenever I'd throw them the ball, they'd put it in the damn hole."

Well, that's no help.

Sharman was there first. He won the first of his four titles in 1957, the year before Jones got to Boston. In fact, Jones was not happy that the Celtics had drafted him because he knew playing time would be tough. Eventually, it was clear that Jones was brought in to succeed Sharman as the team's primary scorer, but Jones had big shoes to fill.

Sharman was a shooter, and he wasn't just dropping set shots. Sharman's form was certainly influenced by the day, but it was pretty obvious that it could translate to today's league pretty easily.

"Hard work and proper technique," Sharman said of his shooting touch. "It all began when my father nailed a basketball hoop to one of our barns in the backyard. And that's where

The early NBA days weren't kind to shooting percentages, but Sharman's shot still looked pure. In a different era, he might have been an even more potent scorer. He was one of the NBA's first true shooters, leading the league in free throw percentage in seven of his 11 NBA seasons. (WIKIMEDIA COMMONS)

I'd be most of the time ... Grasping the basic fundamentals sparked my love and passion for the game."

In fact, Sharman would probably fit very well in today's "let it fly" NBA. He would certainly be capable of hitting from 3-point range, and his mentality wouldn't limit how much he shot.

"I don't like to hear that this guy or that guy is a gunner ... and only thinks of himself ... or that all shooters are selfish players," Sharman told the *Sporting News* in 1958. "I'm a shooter. I'm paid to shoot. He helps the team by shooting. Take Russell's case. Does he say to one of us. 'I'll take this rebound and you take the next?' Certainly not. He gets all the rebounds he can. That's his job and he's helping the team."

Sharman's shot was so pure, he led the NBA in free throw shooting in seven of his 11 years in the NBA. He averaged 17.8 points per game, but had a three-year stretch where he averaged 21.1, 22.3, and 20.4 points per game. His career playoff average climbed to 18.5 points per game, with four seasons that topped 20 points per game in the playoffs.

"Cousy made the game easy for me," Sharman once said. "He was like Larry Bird, in that he knew what was going to happen before anyone else did. My job was to get open. If I did that I knew he would get me the ball."

Back in Sharman's days, shooting percentages were very low. In 1953, when he first led the NBA in free throw percentage (at 85 percent), he shot 43.6 percent from the field. That was still good for second in the league. So while his overall shooting numbers might not compare with some others, he was generally pretty good for his era.

If we're looking for strikes against Sharman, you can look no further than the 1971-72 season. Oh, it's nothing he did on the court. He retired from the Celtics in 1961. However, Sharman did commit one cardinal sin in Boston.

Thou shalt not help the Los Angeles Lakers in any way ever.

And so it was, in the year 1972 anno domini, that Sharman violated this code and coached the dastardly Lakers to an NBA championship. For this sin, Sharman is subject to a stern finger-wagging and a squinty side-eye.

In reality, Sharman could have become the Lakers' Red Auerbach and it wouldn't have mattered much in this debate. Sharman was a very good basketball player for the Celtics, but Sam Jones was just better.

When Jones broke through, he did it in a big way. His career scoring average is 17.7, but he didn't score much in those overlapping years with Sharman. In fact, he averaged 11 points per game in his four seasons with Sharman on the team and 20.8 points once he took over the lead shooting guard spot.

In his first season without Sharman, Jones averaged 18.4 points per game, and his peak run of 25.9, 23.5, 22.1, and 21.3 points per game averages from 1965 to 1968 was more dominant than Sharman had ever been. Even in an era when shooting percentages were low, Jones shot 45.6 percent for his career, a number Sharman only reached once. Even factoring in free throws, where Sharman has Jones beat by eight percentage points, Jones has a better career true shooting percentage.

In his third year with the Celtics, Auerbach bestowed a special honor on Jones.

He gave him the green light to shoot the basketball, which was not given to just anyone. A player had to earn Auerbach's trust with his scoring ability. He had to prove to Auerbach that he was worthy of freelancing outside a set offense, and Jones had done that.

"I said, 'Coach, what did you say?'" Jones told author Michael McClellan. "He said, 'You've got the green light, and that gives you a lot of responsibility.' So I felt kind of special then."

As the final nail in this debate, Jones had a monster seven-year run of 20-plus points per game scoring averages in the

1960 WORLD CHAMPION BOSTON CELTICS

Hailed as the greatest team in the entire history of basketball, this aggregation won 59 of 75 games—17 of them in succession—and repeated as champions for the second straight season. Sitting (left to right) Frank Ramsey, Capt. Bob Cousy, Coach Red Auerbach, President Walter A. Brown, Treasurer Louis A. R. Pieri, K. C. Jones, Bill Sharman. Standing: Gene Guarilia, Tommy Heinsohn, John Richter, Bill Russell, Gene Conley, Jim Loscutoff, Sam Jones and Trainer Edward (Buddy) LeRoux.   (Photo, Buckley)

The look on Sam Jones's face probably gave away his feelings about being on this particular Celtics team in 1960. His career didn't take off for another couple of years, but when it did, he earned the nickname "Mr. Clutch" and he became one of the best scorers in team history. (WIKIMEDIA COMMONS)

playoffs. In fact, Jones's first playoffs without Sharman was the first of those seven years.

Sharman has Jones beat in the accolades department, but that can be misleading as Jones had to compete with Oscar Robertson and Jerry West. Jones only made three All-NBA teams, all of them second-team selections, while Sharman had four first-team and three second-team All-NBA selections. Jones played in five All-Star Games to Sharman's eight.

Jones has more rings than Sharman, though. More than twice as many, in fact. Jones is one of only three Celtics (along with Russell and K. C. Jones) to play on all eight of Boston's consecutive championships in the 1960s. Jones won championships in all but two years of his NBA career.

He's one of only five Boston Celtics to ever score 50 points in a game. His 51 points on October 29, 1965, is the fifth-highest single-game scoring output in Boston Celtics history. He's Boston's sixth all-time leading scorer. Jones's best single scoring season produced 2,070 points. In fact his top six scoring seasons are better than Sharman's best.

I don't need to add anything to this argument.

So I'll let Bill Russell do it for me again.

"In the years that I played with the Celtics," Russell once said, "in terms of total basketball skills, Sam Jones was the most skillful player that I ever played with."

Six times during Boston's run of eight straight championships, the Celtics threw Jones the ball and asked him to take a season-saving shot. All six times, Jones came through, preserving perhaps the greatest championship streak in all of sports.

Jones saved his best for last, nailing a buzzer-beater off the wrong foot to win Game 4 of the 1969 NBA Finals against the Los Angeles Lakers. It was the 35-year-old Jones's final season, and one final chance to send the Lakers home crying.

The Laker led the series two games to one. A loss would send the series back to Los Angeles with Boston down 3–1, a nearly impossible hill to climb.

With seven seconds to go and the Celtics down one, Bill Russell, then player-coach, called a timeout and drew up one more play for Jones.

"Later, he told me he almost didn't call it because it was my last season and he said that people always remember the one you missed," Jones said. "But I made it, and I knew it was good from the time it left my hand. It rolled right over the cylinder. We won the game and went on to win the championship."

He finished the final three games of that series shooting 25-for-45, including a 24-point, 10-for-16 performance in Game 7, his final game as a Celtic.

Jones is one of the most clutch players in team history. He's knocked off his former teammate to move into the lead for this All-Time All-Star honor, but is there another player more deserving in the team's more modern history?

REGGIE LEWIS

In a different universe, Reggie Lewis would have made this an incredibly difficult debate.

Lewis was a smooth, 6'7" wing with all the tools to be an elite player. He was a late bloomer, which is why he went to Northeastern University in Boston (where he still holds the

Reggie Lewis had a well-rounded game. Over the course of his career, he set highs of 42 points, 12 rebounds, 12 assists, 5 blocks, and 5 steals. (STEVE LIPOFSKY WWW.BASKETBALLPHOTO.COM)

scoring record) rather than one of the schools in a traditional basketball power conference. It's why he was available to Boston with the 22nd pick in 1987.

His rookie season was uneventful, but he averaged 19.2 points per game over the next five years of his career, including one All-Star season. He averaged 20.8 over his final two seasons. He had a remarkable four-year run where he averaged 20.3, 20.2, 22.4, and 22.8 points per game in the playoffs. That alone matches up extraordinarily well with others in this debate.

"Reggie was hard to stop," Larry Bird once told the great Jackie MacMullan. "He kept you off balance all the time. There were a few guys in the league I hated to guard because you didn't know what they were thinking.

"I'm glad Reggie was my teammate, because he was one of them."

Former Detroit Piston Joe Dumars is one of the most respected defenders in NBA history. He was so good, he made a *Sports Illustrated* cover where he was heralded as the Michael Jordan stopper. When he was asked which non-Jordan player he hated defending most, he chose Reggie Lewis.

"He was long, athletic, smooth, he could raise up over you and shoot," he told Zach Lowe, then of Grantland. "Man, he was a tough guy to guard. He was definitely the one, other than MJ, who was the toughest for me to figure out. He was so long, and you couldn't really get physical with him, because he was so slim, and it always seemed like I was getting called for fouls. He was a great, great player."

Not only was Lewis a spectacular offensive player, he was a pretty damn good defender too. His signature defensive moment came against Jordan in 1991, when he became the only player to ever block Jordan four times in a game. His long arms and athleticism allowed him to recover and make plays when an offensive player thought he was in the clear.

Sadly, a heart condition led to his death at age 27. It's impossible to know how the rest of his career might have gone, but he was on a trajectory to greatness. I have no doubt that had he had a full career, the debate between Lewis and Sam Jones for the second-best shooting guard would have been a rager. There's even an outside chance he could have challenged Havlicek. He was that good.

RAY ALLEN

Ray Allen was also a very good basketball player, and had he spent his entire career in Boston, this would be one of the most hotly debated rankings of any team. He's still a ridiculous athlete thanks to an obsessive workout routine, but the Milwaukee Bucks version of Allen was one of the league's top players and a high-flyer who competed in the 1997 All-Star Weekend dunk contest.

We remember Allen as an aging star who morphed his game to more of a specialist with the Celtics. Sure, he was at the end of his prime when he was traded away from the Seattle Sonics, but he was still a damn good player. He had averaged 26.4 points per game in the year before the trade, the highest scoring average of his career.

He joined the Celtics and, along with Kevin Garnett and Paul Pierce, formed an intimidating new Big 3. Like the first iteration, this trio had its unique personalities.

"He was the even-keeled demeanor of our basketball team, which made us so unique," Paul Pierce told The Undefeated.

Allen was always a great shooter, but he became much more of a
3-point specialist in Boston. He once took 18 3s in a game as a Celtic.
(STEVE LIPOFSKY WWW.BASKETBALLPHOTO.COM)

"KG was really intense. I was kind of in the middle. Then you had Ray to kind of balance us out."

Allen's professionalism was the perfect rudder for a team burning hot with Kevin Garnett's rage and intensity. He helped mold Rajon Rondo, and taught him the benefit of building a routine. Their relationship ultimately deteriorated, but Allen's influence on Rondo in the early days of his career was invaluable.

Allen averaged no fewer than 21.8 points per game in the eight seasons prior to joining the Boston Celtics. He never averaged more than 18.2 with Boston, which is still really good for a guy who spent ages 32 to 36 with the Celtics. However, it's not going to get him close to where he needs to be to make this list.

DANNY AINGE

Danny Ainge is one of the few people in consideration for this team whose number is not retired. What Ainge does have in common with Jones and Sharman is that he was one of Red Auerbach's favorites.

Red loved instigators, aggressive guys who took it to an opponent rather than passive players who waited to retaliate. If some of that aggressiveness spilled into a tussle, fracas, or full-blown donnybrook, so be it. Red would rather have dialed someone back than tried to pull some emotion out of him.

He'd never have that issue with Ainge, who was as fiery on the court as they came. He famously got into a fight with Atlanta Hawks center Tree Rollins in 1983, during which Rollins bit Ainge and inspired the *Boston Herald* headline "Tree Bites Man."

Ainge was an antagonist. He once brought a stethoscope into the locker room before a Finals game to see which of his teammates had heart.
(STEVE LIPOFSKY WWW.BASKETBALLPHOTO.COM)

"The (opposing team's) fans are still gonna boo and call me names. That's their prerogative," Ainge told the *Los Angeles Times*. "What I do is try to use it to my advantage, to motivate me. I'd heard so much about how the fans in Atlanta were going to yell and curse at me when we went down there (during the semifinals), I got all psyched up for them, and they were actually good. Frankly, I was disappointed."

Ainge's best attributes seemed to be taking verbal abuse from his teammates, and keeping things light when he could.

Robert Parish has a great Ainge story about a prank he pulled on legendary radio broadcaster Johnny Most.

In the 1980s teams flew on commercial flights. So even though they flew first class, they shared planes with the general public.

"(Most) was a chainsmoker. He smoked cigarettes, and cigarettes, and cigarettes," Parish said on the Locked On Celtics podcast in 2016. "So Danny Ainge got these, I don't know what you would call them, these candy cigarettes that explode after you light them? They had the explosive tip? And so Danny replaced three or four of Johnny Most's cigarettes with explosive cigarettes. So Johnny Most just slept on every flight. He would just sleep. And so when he woke up, the first thing he did was light up a cigarette. And so he would light up a cigarette, and then it would explode, and he'd be like 'what the M-F-?' and then he would light another cigarette and it would explode and he'd be like 'what M-F- bothered my cigarettes?' And then he'd take out another one and it would explode and he's getting up ranting up and down the walkway. And of course the stewardess would intervene after that because you're not supposed to be walking up and down the aisle throwing a temper tantrum. So we were all just about falling out of our seats with laughter. Everybody thought it was funny but Johnny Most."

Ainge was a key player in two Celtics championships, but he was never "the guy" on any of his teams. He never averaged more than 15.7 points per game as a Celtic, though his career 48.7 percent shooting as a Celtic is an amazing number. He shot 38.6 percent from 3 in Boston, but because that shot was not emphasized as it is today, he only took 1.6 per game.

Ainge was a big part of Boston's success in the 1980s, and maybe he'd make another team's All-Time All-Star list with those numbers, but there have just been too many greats to come through town to crack this one.

Making Jones the choice here just makes too much sense. There's also a synergy with Havlicek as the other two-guard on this team. It was Jones, after all, who caught the ball Havlicek stole. It'd be a travesty not to have them on this team together.

Aside from Sharman, there hasn't been a shooting guard good enough who has been around Boston long enough to supplant those two. Frank Ramsey, whose number 23 is retired by the Celtics, was the original "sixth man" and he won seven titles in Boston, and even he is a bit of an afterthought.

There is one reason to consider Ramsey, at least ironically. Ramsey could be considered the godfather of NBA flopping, having literally penned a manual on how to manipulate officiating to draw fouls.

"Drawing fouls chiefly requires the ability to provide good, heartwarming drama and to direct it to the right audience," he wrote in a 1963 *Sports Illustrated* article under the heading "Why I fall." "I never forget where the referees are when I go into an act. The most reliable eye-catcher is still the pratfall.

Particularly on defense, when everything else fails, I fall down. Luckily I happen to be type-cast for the part because I have a peculiar running style—back on my heels, with my knees locked. It makes falling very easy and natural-looking for me."

This should dispel the notion that flopping arrived in the NBA with the influx of international players who took their cues from ridiculous soccer histrionics. It's been happening since the dawn of the NBA. Ramsey won't make this team, but this contribution to the game should be noted for the record.

Back to those who are actually on this squad.

If Havlicek's career is understated, Jones's is criminally underrated. It's partly because Boston's history is so full of great players. Jones was the leading scorer in the midst of Boston's historic '60s title run, yet all the credit seems to go to Bill Russell.

Ultimately, Havlicek just accomplished a bit more than Jones, even though Jones was the more prolific scorer. Hopefully Jones making Boston's All-Time All-Star team can help him get more of the recognition he deserves.

Final verdict:
Starter: John Havlicek
Backup: Sam Jones

SMALL FORWARD

The Candidates

Cedric Maxwell
Paul Pierce
Larry Bird

The small forward is a jack-of-all-trades position. They are often some of the most dynamic players on the floor because they combine some of the qualities of the point guard and shooting guard with a bit more size, but they still have better mobility than power forwards or centers.

Small forwards are often somewhere between 6'7" and 6'9", which makes them too big to be guards and too small to be big men. Tommy Heinsohn likes to call the position the "quick forward" as a nod to their ability to generally move well for players of that size.

Small forwards can be big scorers, but they can also find themselves under the basket to get rebounds and blocked shots or on the perimeter in position to make passes. Every basketball player tends to be a great athlete, but the small forward tends to combine some of the best attributes of all four other positions.

Now you see why I moved John Havlicek to shooting guard. I just simply wasn't going to leave two of these guys off the team. It's bad enough that one might not make it.

I know what you're thinking.

This decision seems pretty easy!

OK. Yeah. It sort of is, but I want to throw out here that this section includes, perhaps, the three best shit-talkers in team history.

That has to count for something, right?

Maxwell once spent a pregame in Los Angeles putting on a kid's glasses and taking comically ugly shots to mock the bespectacled Kurt Rambis. Pierce famously spent 15 seconds of a clutch playoff possession talking so much trash to Al Harrington that the referee had to stick his head into the play to tell them to shut up. Pierce buried the shot anyway.

And Bird. Whew. Bird was the trash-talkingest trash-talker of them all. He walked into the All-Star locker room before the 3-point shootout and asked "Who's finishing second?" before going out and winning. He played a game mostly left-handed because he was bored.

The best, though, was Bird against the Seattle Supersonics, when he trash-talked in his own huddle then called his shot.

The C's and Sonics were tied with 13 seconds left. As K. C. Jones drew up a play, Bird told him, "Why don't you give me the ball and tell everyone to get out of my way."

When he broke the huddle, he went to Xavier McDaniel, who drew the defensive assignment, and told him, "I'm going to get the ball right here, and I'm going to hit the shot right in your face."

Kendrick Perkins overtook Max's career numbers, but his 1980 season is still the best shooting season in team history. (STEVE LIPOFSKY WWW .BASKETBALLPHOTO.COM)

When he did with two seconds left, he turned to McDaniel and said, "I didn't mean to leave any time on the clock."

Brutal. That's a bad man at work. But as much fun as the trash-talking is, it's no good if it's not backed up, and these guys backed up just about every word. Still we can only have two of them on the team, and it's pretty clear who they'll be.

So this section is less about debate and more about celebration of greatness. It's also about just how many damn good players have worn the Celtics green over the course of their lives.

CEDRIC MAXWELL

Think about it. We're all just casually dismissing Cedric Maxwell, a two-time champion and a Finals MVP. He twice led the league and still leads the team in field goal percentage. He was a really good basketball player and without him, it's possible Boston doesn't win either of those titles.

Maxwell's stellar career started at UNC-Charlotte (where his jersey is retired, and a teammate gave him the "Cornbread" nickname because he thought Max reminded him of a movie character with the same name). He was drafted 12th overall by the Celtics in 1977. He broke out in his sophomore season in Boston to lead the team in scoring (19 ppg), field goal percentage (58.4 percent), rebounding (9.9 rpg), and free throw attempts and makes.

Max had little help in what was a very difficult season. The arrival of Larry Bird helped the Celtics turn things around, and the moves that brought Kevin McHale and Robert Parish created the group we affectionately know as "the Big 3."

But Maxwell was the team's third-leading scorer that year and their second-leading scorer in the playoffs. In the 1981 Finals, it was Maxwell who took over to lead the Celtics to victory and earn the Finals MVP. He was always among the Celtics top scorers and best shooters, but always overlooked as the Big 3 became the team's focal point.

Max went from the team's star to a supporting player in a hurry, but he had one more bit of magic up his sleeve before things fell apart for him in Boston. As the story goes, Maxwell told his teammates to climb on his back before dominating Game 7 of the 1984 Finals against the Lakers. His 24-point, 8-rebound, 8-assist game clinched his second title, and Boston's 15th.

Cornbread was a hero once again, but then it fell apart.

He suffered a knee injury in the 1984-85 season that caused a significant rift with the team. Red Auerbach essentially called him lazy. His work ethic was questioned. And when Maxwell sat out in Game 6 of the 1985 Finals, a loss to the Lakers, he knew his time in Boston was over.

"I remember myself, M. L. Carr, and Quinn Buckner looking at each other and knowing that we would not be back the following year: we shed some tears," he would say about that game.

The Celtics essentially blamed Maxwell for the loss. While Max said he just couldn't play, the team thought he was bailing on them, which drove a wedge between them.

"The most upsetting thing about that was questioning my integrity. That was very upsetting," Max would say in an NBC Sports documentary. "The crazy part about it was there were still four guys who were Hall of Famers. And I think if there was one thing that I felt was why did I have to be the scapegoat?

"I understood we were trying to win a championship. I understood that was important to the cause. But I was going to get healed and I was going to be well in God's time. Not Red Auerbach's time, not the Celtics' time, but in God's time. And it just took longer than I wanted and they wanted, and that was just really bad."

From there Maxwell and Auerbach stubbornly squared off in a battle of wills. Max passed on Auerbach's invitation to attend the Celtics' rookie camp and test his knee. In the book *The Last Banner*, Maxwell admits he acted like a stubborn kid stomping his feet and refusing to go. But he also blames Red.

Maxwell wasn't just moved out of town, he was sent to what he called NBA Siberia . . . the Clippers. Auerbach went so far as to remove complimentary references to Maxwell from his most recent book. To Red, Maxwell was a distant memory, happily discarded for Bill Walton, who helped the Celtics win their 16th title.

It cut Maxwell deeply.

"When Red said the things he said after I left, it bothered me," Maxwell told the *Boston Globe*. "It was like he was trying to hurt me. Red has the greatest basketball mind that there's ever been, but I just don't think that was fair at the end. I don't think the way it was done was the best. They said things about me, about my integrity, and that's what bothered me. After everything I had done, they questioned my desire to win. I was involved in two championships and had a lot to do with winning. And to say I didn't care, and didn't have a desire to come back, was unfair."

Racial issues also tinged Maxwell's time in Boston. The arrival of Larry Bird, and the city's embracing of him, highlighted a divide which Maxwell was more than willing to discuss.

"The Celtics are a business organization. If they can put more fans in the seats by putting all white players on the team, they would do that, but they have great black players, so that's not going to happen. I knew there was going to be a certain balance, but that's justified from a financial standpoint. If there's going to be one last player on the bench, a black or a white, what's the difference?

"I enjoyed playing in Boston. It was a great team and a great place to play. I loved the Garden fans. It's not that anybody hated playing there. We enjoyed playing for the team. But you always had a certain atmosphere there. Why were there never any endorsements for the black guys—other than M. L. (Carr), who is the perfect example of assimilation? He can be a chameleon. But we had me and DJ (Dennis Johnson) and Robert (Parish), and we weren't getting any offers and guys like Rick Robey were. Why was that happening? Did you ever see me on TV? That's just evident."

I bring this up to highlight Max's openness to talk about anything and say things as he sees them. What came off as a complaint or criticism was often said as "this is how I see things." Boston was only a few years removed from violent protests amidst its busing crisis. The historically white NBA had merged with the mostly Black ABA while he was in college.

It was a complex time in the city and the league. Racial issues were prevalent. Maxwell saw it, felt it, and ultimately spoke about it.

Time, as they say, heals all wounds, and it certainly did with Maxwell and the Celtics. A reconciliation between him and Red helped repair the relationship between him and the team. Once Red was ready to move on, Max extended the olive branch, and ultimately apologized to Auerbach for his handling of the situation.

For many years, it seemed Maxwell was destined for a life as the overlooked star in Boston's storied history. In many ways, he still is. But now, we can appreciate Maxwell for who he was rather than the misconception many had of him after his acrimonious departure.

Max was a talker on the court who wasn't shy to let anyone have it. Before his knee injury, he'd back it up with a practically unstoppable game within five feet of the hoop.

He's a Finals MVP and part of two champions in Boston. He's a guy who loves to talk and loves to have fun with his job as listeners to the Celtics radio broadcasts, on which he provided color commentary, will attest.

It was a rocky road for Maxwell, but it ultimately led him home. His number 31 is retired, and until the retirement of Paul Pierce's 34, it was the most recent of the numbers to go up into the rafters.

Just like Pierce bumped him from that distinction, he'll bump Maxwell from this one as well.

PAUL PIERCE

Pierce is behind only Havlicek on the Celtics scoring list. He scored 24,021 with the Celtics, but if you add the 2,376 he scored after his trade away from Boston, he finished his career with two more points than Hondo.

Paul Pierce finished his career with more points than John Havlicek, and his peak numbers compared pretty favorably to Kobe Bryant's.
(KEITH ALLISON VIA WIKIMEDIA COMMONS, STEVE LIPOFSKY WWW.BASKETBALL PHOTO.COM)

He's a 10-time All-Star, a Finals MVP, a four-time All-NBA player. He's the Celtics all-time leader in 3-pointers taken and made, free throws taken and made, and steals. He's fifth in team history in assists, and seventh in rebounds.

Pierce would be on the list of best Celtics of all time regardless of position. What makes Pierce extra special is his story. Perhaps the most endearing thing about Pierce is how he went from people wanting him out of town to one of the city's most adored athletes.

It's hard to find a more perfect character in the NBA's story than Paul Pierce. From beginning to end, nearly every detail of his career was crafted so beautifully it's as if each sprung divinely from a playwright's pen to maximize the dramatic effect.

Like most good stories, his begins benignly. He was a McDonald's All-American out of high school. He went to a basketball powerhouse in Kansas. After three years (the norm at the time), he left school early in 1998 and was expected to be no worse than a top-five pick.

And then . . .

The top five pick slipped to sixth.

Then seventh.

Then eighth.

The Celtics were so enamored with Dirk Nowitzki that we wouldn't be here right now if this was where they picked. They took great pains to hide their interest and keep any word of Nowitzki's existence from the media. It was the pre-YouTube era, and their plan seemed to be falling into place. What they didn't know is the Dallas Mavericks had the same idea.

Dallas selected ninth.

By the time the Boston Celtics were on the clock, the best player on the board was a lifelong Lakers fan from Inglewood, California. The kid who'd snuck into games at the Fabulous Forum to watch Showtime and boo the Boston Celtics was suddenly shaking David Stern's hand with a green hat on his head.

"Inside, my body cringed," Pierce said of draft night. "I was like 'a Celtic? C'mon.' Rick Pitino running you into the dirt, Celtics I hated growing up."

Initially, the stage wasn't even his in Boston. That belonged to Pitino, the college star lured back to the NBA to help save the franchise. It was a team rocked by two deaths and a tank job that didn't accomplish its goal of landing Tim Duncan. Pitino was supposed to end a title drought that lasted more than a decade . . . more than twice as long as any other in team history.

They had a lot of work to do.

Pierce did very well in his first two years, but the team didn't. The pressure was mounting on Pitino and the Celtics to show some results.

On September 25, 2000, just before the beginning of his third season, Paul Pierce walked into the Buzz Club on Stuart Street with teammate Tony Battie and a few others.

A fight broke out.

Pierce intervened.

A bottle was smashed on his head. He was stabbed 11 times in the face, neck, and back.

Two things helped keep Pierce alive. His leather jacket, which helped minimize the damage just enough, and the quick-thinking Battie who rushed him to the Tufts Medical Center just blocks away.

If this had happened at a different club, or had Pierce made a different choice in wardrobe, he very well might have died that night. Instead, he made it into surgery. A punctured lung was repaired. The wounds were stitched. And just one month later, Pierce was on the floor for opening night.

Pierce was the only Celtic to make it through all 82 games that season. Pitino left halfway through the year, leaving Pierce to pick up the pieces of another failed rebuild.

These next few years are a very important part of the Paul Pierce story. Between 2002 and 2006 Pierce slid perilously close to becoming a Boston sports villain.

Pierce made his first All-Star team in 2002. He led the NBA in total points and was third in points per game. He helped get the Celtics to the Conference Finals and led a miracle comeback against Jason Kidd's New Jersey Nets in the third game of a series they'd ultimately lose.

Pierce was riding high enough to be selected to represent Team USA in the 2002 World Championships. He played well enough to cruise through the first few games.

And then things fell apart. Team USA didn't even medal and Pierce took the brunt of the blame, especially from head coach George Karl.

"When we got beat and were told to be humble and take our losses like warriors, he decided to jump out there and fight the negativity. And because I was the head man, I had to call him out on it," Karl said at the time. "None of us wanted to play those last two games. None of us wanted to watch film. But you've got to do that. And Paul just pushed the line, pushed the line. His reaction to the negativity, to a crisis, was that we all have to protect ourselves, our own egos."

Pierce had just committed the cardinal sin of leading a USA Basketball team to a non-medal finish in international play. He would return to Boston with a rich new contract but a reputation as a selfish, petulant star. He was "part of the problem" in a wild new era of NBA basketball.

It should be noted that this was at the same time hip-hop and the NBA got married. In 2001, Reebok and Nike released iconic hip-hop-themed commercials. Allen Iverson dribbled behind Jadakiss to sell us A5s while Pierce appeared in a Nike Freestyle commercial. Hip-hop culture entered the popular culture, and it caused a significant divide between younger fans and NBA "lifers."

Many young players were branded as thugs. The NBA instituted a dress code. Many people's view of NBA stars, Pierce included, was tainted.

The next two seasons saw more frustration, dwindling playoff success, another coaching change, and the lowest point of Pierce's Celtics career.

The Doc Rivers–led Celtics went 45-37, winning the division and earning the third seed in the playoffs and a date with the Indiana Pacers in the first round.

In the waning minutes of Game 6, with the Celtics down three games to two, Pierce was hit in the face by Jamaal Tinsley. There was no call, and Pierce swung his arm, sending Tinsley to the floor. Pierce picked up his second technical foul, and was ejected from the game. On his way off the floor, Pierce took his jersey off and swung it over his head as he left.

After the game, he showed up to the postgame news conference with his head ridiculously wrapped in athletic gauze to highlight that he hadn't gotten the foul call he wanted. His complaining was off-putting. The Celtics won the game but lost the series. More importantly, Pierce lost a lot of fans in Boston.

This could have been the end of the Paul Pierce story. Hell, it almost was. The Celtics nearly traded him for Chris Paul on draft night that June.

But they couldn't.

Pierce was going to come back, even though there were very loud calls to trade him away. Everyone knew something had to change.

"I just had to go home and grow up," acknowledged Pierce. "It was a difficult situation. It was time to grow up, stop pouting, go out there and help these young guys out and things will work out. And that was my mind-set after the first year with Doc [Rivers]. So that was my attitude after that and I think that helped out my relationship with Doc and them wanting to keep me around because they saw the change in my attitude. Trying to get better as a Celtic regardless of the losing that was going on here."

Redemption is powerful. When you see a glimmer of light in someone who's in a dark place, you begin to root for salvation.

For Pierce it began with a conversation with Rivers in which he rededicated himself to the team. He returned to have his best season in 2005-06, but the team was still bad. He missed most of the following year due to injury and, frustrated, he again questioned his future in Boston.

This time, though, Danny Ainge's plan was to build a winner around Pierce. While bad lottery luck cost Ainge his first option, drafting Kevin Durant, he took the fifth pick and flipped it for Ray Allen. He then got Kevin Garnett in a blockbuster trade, and Paul Pierce suddenly, finally, was on a contender.

Pierce, more than anyone else, sacrificed his game for the greater good. He still won games with his signature right-elbow step-back jumper, but he also let Garnett and Allen do their things. He took over when needed and ceded the spotlight if it was right.

There was just one thing left to do.

Ten years after the lifelong Lakers fan became a Celtic, the lifelong Celtic had one more obstacle to clear so he could finish writing his perfect NBA story.

The Los Angeles Lakers.

Beating the Lakers is a rite of passage for every Celtics legend. The moment Pierce crossed this threshold, he transformed.

He wasn't that petulant kid anymore. He wasn't the guy who torpedoed Team USA or the childish star in a bandage.

As Paul Pierce stood on a rickety table at center court, pumping the Finals MVP trophy over his head while staffers held his stage desperately trying to keep it steady, Pierce became a Celtics legend.

"When I first got to the Celtics I didn't know what to think," he said. "My initial thought was like no, not the Celtics. That's because I hated them, I hated that they beat the Lakers a couple of times. And as I got more and more engulfed in the history of what the Celtics were about, what the pride was all about, I fell in love with it. It was like this is what basketball should be about for every franchise."

It's unfortunate that he couldn't finish his career in Boston, but the cold-hearted business of the NBA forced Ainge's hand. As if giving the team one last buzzer-beating win, Pierce, along with Kevin Garnett, left Boston in one of the most lopsided trades in NBA history. It's a move still paying off in 2020, with

Jaylen Brown and Jayson Tatum, both selected with picks that came from the Brooklyn Nets, as cornerstones for the franchise's future.

LARRY BIRD

Larry Bird isn't just a cornerstone in Celtics history; he's part of the foundation on which the modern NBA was built.

Bird is such an interesting person because in so many ways he's still "the hick from French Lick." In so many others he's one of the league's most vicious assassins. He's the ultimate "kids today don't get it" player because in today's NBA of chiseled physiques, Bird just looks like some dude with a bad mustache waiting for next at your men's league game.

What he was, however, was not only one of the best players in team history, but one of the best the league has ever seen. If the Hall of Fame had a Hall of Fame, he'd be in it.

Bird, along with Magic Johnson, helped save the NBA. It's hard to say what would have happened to the league had he not existed, but it feels safe to say life would have been a lot different.

In 1979, Bird entered a league riddled with drug problems, apathetic fans, and lacking a spotlight. When he left it, the game had gone global and influenced a generation that gave rise to today's international stars. He and Magic didn't do it alone, but they kicked down the door and led the charge.

The Celtics also reasserted their dominance over that time, and rekindled a special rivalry with the Los Angeles Lakers. I don't need to list his resume here, but it sure is fun to look at.

He's a three-time NBA MVP and a three-time champion. He was named to 10 All-NBA teams, three All-Defensive

This exact free throw pose was used by sculptor Armand LaMontagne for his famous wood statue of Bird, which now can be seen in the upper ring of the TD Garden. (STEVE LIPOFSKY WWW.BASKETBALLPHOTO .COM)

teams, and 12 All-Star teams (winning one All-Star MVP). He was the Rookie of the Year. He's a Hall of Famer.

He averaged 24.3 points per game for his career and his scoring average fell below 20 in only one season (1990-91, when he averaged 19.6). He shot nearly 50 percent for his career, 37.6 percent on 3-pointers, and 88.6 percent from the free throw line. He rarely rested in the playoffs, averaging 42 minutes per game and winning two NBA Finals MVPs.

He's obviously a starter on this All-Time All-Star team. Not only that, he's in the debate for the best player on this team. Frankly, that it is even a debate shows you how ridiculous the talent level has been in Boston.

It's funny how close he came to not even being a basketball player.

To understand Bird, as much as anyone can, is to understand how he grew up. Bird spent his childhood in relative poverty outside French Lick, Indiana. His father, Joe, worked hard when he could find work, but was an alcoholic. His mother, Georgia, worked to make up the difference.

Growing up with little taught him what was really important in life. He rarely got caught up in outside trappings or sought the spotlight. Watching his mom work countless hours and his dad pull a boot up over a badly injured ankle burned the importance of a work ethic into his brain.

Growing up in a small town taught him to know people. He learned what made them tick. He could tell who was genuine, and who the bullshitters were. This was especially important for Bird as he navigated racial issues throughout his life and career.

A young Larry Bird turned to sports with his brothers to pass the time, but as he grew up in age and height, basketball started to nudge ahead in his athletic pecking order. Once he realized he could be good at it, and, maybe just as importantly, could find friendship and fulfillment from it, he fell in love.

As a teenager, he'd find games where he could, and the best competition he could find was against the predominantly Black hotel workers near his childhood home. Race relations were tense in the late 1960s and early 1970s but it didn't matter in these games. Everyone got along through basketball.

"They treated me very well," Bird said in an interview with The Undefeated. "When I showed up, if somebody needed a break, they'd throw me right in there and I'd be in there the rest of the day. But they were pretty good players. They really weren't great by any means. They always seemed to let me get in there and play with them, and I always enjoyed that because I always looked at that group of guys. They had a great kinship, they got along very well. . . . Score meant very little, but a lot of talking going on, a lot of fun."

Maybe the best way to describe Bird is that he likes things simple. That's why these games were fun to him; it was just a bunch of guys having fun playing ball and nothing else mattered. The more complicated things got for Bird, the less comfortable he got.

That probably isn't the best trait for a basketball star in Indiana, where high school stars become celebrities and in-state stars who stay in-state for college are heroes.

Bird became one of those stars, and he committed to Indiana University, but the whole thing fell apart almost instantly.

He was overwhelmed there and hated everything almost immediately, so he left.

This is where Bird could have just faded into anonymity for the rest of his life. He took a maintenance job in French Lick that included work on a garbage truck, and he was happy again.

"I loved that job," Bird once told *Sports Illustrated*. "It was outdoors, you were around your friends. Picking up brush, cleaning up. I felt like I was really accomplishing something. How many times are you riding around your town and you say to yourself, Why don't they fix that? Why don't they clean the streets up? And here I had the chance to do that. I had the chance to make my community look better."

Life was anything but simple, though. His father committed suicide, and Bird decided to go back to school. He chose the smaller Indiana State, which fit Bird's personality better. This time he stuck around, even after a disastrous relationship that ended with a quick marriage and divorce and a daughter before he even stepped on the court.

Bird played three years at Indiana State and grew into stardom as his Sycamores became a national story. By the time he'd lost to Magic and Michigan State, he was ready for the next level.

Even then, Red Auerbach's shrewdness nearly cost the Celtics their future star. He'd drafted Bird in his junior year, and balked at paying Bird his demanded $1 million salary as a rookie. With a threat to enter the 1979 draft and take away Boston's rights to sign him, both sides settled at $650,000 for his rookie season, the richest NBA rookie contract ever at the time.

Bird dominated almost instantly. He averaged 21.3 points per game, became an All-Star, and won Rookie of the Year, beating out Magic Johnson. Magic, though, won the NBA championship with his Los Angeles Lakers that year, and suddenly the rivalry that started in college leapt to the NBA.

It was perfect, really. Bird had his foil in Magic, perhaps the only other player in the league who could match his talent and drive him as a peer. Bird, the small-town, blue-collar, winning-over-everything star fit perfectly in Boston while Magic and his giant personality and ego went to Showtime in Los Angeles, the Celtics' biggest rival.

There was a racial element to this as well. Bird was billed by some in the media as Boston's "Great White Hope." Boston's own history played into this, as it was accepted as fact that the city's predominantly white fans rushed back to the team they'd written off because it now had a white star.

The day he walked into training camp, he was tested by Cedric Maxwell. Bird quickly hit shot after shot, from farther and farther away, quickly establishing that he not only belonged, but was better than anyone else on the floor.

"Max was doing a lot of talking. But the day I walked in there, you know, it was interesting what happened," Bird said in his Undefeated interview. "When I went to my first practice they had Sidney Wicks and Curtis Rowe, which I didn't know him personally, but I remember watching them on TV at UCLA. Then you had Maxwell. The only time I ever heard of his name was when I went to Boston to watch a game. I didn't even know who he was. When I walked in, there he was, doing a lot of talking.

"By the time our first practice was over, Curtis and Sidney both were cut, and Max is the only one left. You go into these things and go, well, you don't know how you're going to be treated, but I ain't taking no shit. If they want to go, we have to go. But Curtis and Sidney were really nice guys. Cedric was doing all the talking. So, second practice, them two were gone and it was just Cedric. And it didn't take long to get him quiet."

Maxwell famously recalled that, in that moment, he thought to himself "damn, that white boy can play."

Bird's ambivalence to such things carried him through what would probably be tense moments for other players. When, in 1987, Isiah Thomas said Bird "would just be another good guy" if he was Black, Bird shrugged it off. He legitimately didn't care then and he doesn't care now.

Bird's focus was always on basketball. He seethed, even as he won Rookie of the Year, when Magic and the Lakers won the title in his first year. The idea of Johnson possibly outworking him drove him to work even harder at improving his own game. Magic felt the same way. Their obsession with each other is part of what made their rivalry so great.

They became friends while shooting a sneaker commercial, but the rivalry that drove Bird didn't subside. He took joy in testing himself against the greats of the game. He lived for the biggest moments and loved when new bars were set for him, even if it was a teammate who did it.

In March of 1985, Kevin McHale set the Celtics single-game scoring record by dropping 56 points on the Detroit Pistons. He left the game with about a minute and a half on the clock and the game in hand. Bird, being Bird, told McHale he should have stayed in the game to get 60.

Nine days later, Bird did.

This might be the ultimate Larry Bird story when you think about it.

First, there's his competitiveness. A teammate set a record, and Bird's reaction was oh I have to break this now.

When asked by ESPN when he knew he'd score 60, he said, "I knew I had it when Kevin McHale scored 56 a couple weeks before. I knew I was gonna get there one day."

Second, there's his work ethic and lunacy. They were 64 games into the season and had three days off. Did he rest?

Nope. He ran a five-mile charity road race!

Third, he got to rip an opponent to shreds.

"He told us at halftime that nobody could stop him so just give him the ball and get out of the way," Robert Parish told Boston.com. "Then he went out and started taunting the Atlanta players on the floor, the ones on the bench, their coaches, even the referees. He was talking so much trash he was buried in it. It was one of those nights when he could have drop-kicked the ball in. I loved it."

By the end, the Atlanta Hawks players sitting on the bench were laughing and celebrating Bird's shots as much as anyone. They celebrated so much that Hawks coach Mike Fratello fined the players for their reactions.

What really is the capper for this Bird story and makes it so perfect is that he hates this game. It's one of the best scoring nights in NBA history and the best ever for a Celtic, and Bird doesn't care for it.

"Sixty points is a lot, don't get me wrong. I made shots against the Hawks that game I can't recall making in any other time. It's not easy to do," Bird told Boston.com. "But there was a game from a little earlier that season where I had a triple-double and a bunch of steals in around 30 minutes against the Jazz. That had it all. That was what I'd call a great game."

His favorite game was Game 6 of the 1986 NBA Finals, a game in which he felt he could do anything he wanted. We could go through all the duels he won that made him the Miyamoto Musashi of the NBA. But his best single moment came in 1987.

It's odd that the greatest play by one of the greatest scorers ever was a steal. Even though Bird made three All-Defensive teams, no one was looking to him to lock players down.

But this steal . . . *the* steal . . . this was about awareness and the desire to win. Defense wasn't what Bird was about, but this play was.

Forgotten by history is what led up to the steal, which came in Game 5 of the Eastern Conference Finals.

With the series tied at two games apiece and Boston down one in the waning seconds, the ball was in Bird's hands. He drove left, dribbled along the baseline, and got swallowed up. His shot attempt was swatted away and it went out of bounds off a teammate.

For a fleeting second, a feeling of dread hung over the Garden.

It was sort of like Princess Buttercup in *The Princess Bride* when the priest says, "man and wife," and she turns, wide-eyed, and says, "He didn't come."

"He didn't win the game."

But Bird, like Westley, had his own "never happened" moment, and his fight with the Detroit Pistons was definitely "to the pain."

Isiah Thomas was in such a hurry to inbound the ball and get out of Boston with their win that he never noticed that Bird was only mostly dead. Thomas lofted a pass toward Bill Laimbeer and Bird sprung. At the same time, Dennis Johnson cut to the basket.

This is another unheralded part of this play.

Bird not only stole it, he spun, balanced himself long enough to keep from falling out of bounds, and he fired a pass to the cutting Johnson for the go-ahead bucket. We call this play "the steal," but it was also "the pass" and "the finish."

"That play ranks as the greatest that I've ever been a part of," said Johnson, who once hit a game-winning shot in the 1984 Finals. "We were so hard to beat at home, and anytime you have Larry on your team you feel like you've got a chance, no matter how bad the outlook. Larry made a great play, and I reacted to it."

The absolute best part, the part that makes it dusty in whatever room I'm in, is when Johnson calls Bird over for their hug afterwards.

Instead of going back to Detroit down 3–2, Boston was up. In a flash, the series completely changed.

This play would never happen today because of replays and reviews. Detroit wouldn't have had to call their timeout; the officials would have done it for them.

That makes this play even more outstanding, because there's a good chance it might never be duplicated. Just like Bird. There'll never be another like him.

If there's any one drawback to Bird's legacy, it's that the damn fool hurt himself building a retaining wall. The back issues lingered for the rest of his career. And if that reads like

I'm angry it's only because I'm mad that I didn't get more Larry Bird in my life.

Sue me. I'm greedy like that.

It's probably for the best. Bird was the right guy at the right time. He'd probably be miserable in today's social media atmosphere. He'd probably get crushed for some of the things he did, like allegedly hurting his hand in a bar fight during the 1985 playoffs.

It's best that the legend rests the way it does right now.

We got Bird for 13 years in Boston. Even when there was chatter, some of it even coming from his teammate and current president of basketball operations Danny Ainge, that Boston should move in a different direction, Bird stayed. He wanted to finish his career in Boston and so did Auerbach. Bird admired Auerbach's loyalty.

"That's why he was so successful building and rebuilding those Celtic championship teams," Bird said. "I'm thankful that it worked out that way. I got to play with some great players. We won three championships and came close in a few others. I wanted to retire as a Boston Celtic. I'm very proud of that."

Larry Bird is arguably the greatest Celtic of all time, though I'm not going to force myself to choose between him and Bill Russell. They can be co-captains of this All-Time All-Star team as far as I'm concerned.

Final verdict:
Starter: Larry Bird
Backup: Paul Pierce

POWER FORWARD

The Candidates
Tommy Heinsohn
Kevin Garnett
Kevin McHale

A power forward is traditionally much closer to a center than he is to a small forward. Before the positionless revolution of today's NBA, power forwards were often 6'8"–6'10" versions of centers: big guys who played with their backs to the basket. They often added a bit of a face-up game and maybe a 10-foot jumper to their repertoires, but that's as far out as they'd go.

The power forward spot has changed a lot over the years as players evolved and added more perimeter play to their games. It makes this position varied and unique. Old-school power forwards might be the players who would have the most trouble adjusting to today's NBA.

Nowadays the Celtics are asking Jaylen Brown, normally a 6'6" wing, to play that spot at times and he does it well. If Brown was transported back to the '80s, he'd be a small forward or a shooting guard. Now, with "small-ball" becoming a more regular approach by teams who value positional versatility over traditional roles, what we've known power forwards to be has changed.

Mostly, the "power" part of it is gone. Some of the game's best and most notorious power forwards were strong enforcers, rarely serving as a primary scorer and more in games to defend and commit hard fouls.

Those days are gone, and people like me who appreciated a little on-court policing will miss them. But because that was the case throughout most of basketball history, there aren't a lot of power forwards that rise up to make this an extended debate.

TOMMY HEINSOHN

Heinsohn is the Boston Celtics. If anyone actually bleeds green, it's him.

His Hall of Fame career started in 1956, when the Celtics took him with their territorial selection. Back then, when the NBA was just getting going, teams were allowed to draft players from local colleges regardless of their actual draft position. The theory was local fans would follow their college stars to their NBA team, thus growing interest.

Let's just pause for a quick second to talk about this 1956 draft, in which Boston not only got Heinsohn, but also Bill Russell and K. C. Jones. Three Hall of Famers: the Rookie of the Year, the greatest winner of all time, and one of the fiercest defenders the league has ever seen. And all it cost Boston was the Ice Capades. (If you don't know what I'm talking about, you'll have to read the Bill Russell section.)

Anyway, Heinsohn was a star at Holy Cross a couple of years after Bob Cousy left, setting single-game and career

Tommy Heinsohn is the only person in Celtics history to experience every one of the team's championships. He won eight as a player, two as a coach, and was a broadcaster for the remaining seven. (WIKIMEDIA COMMONS)

scoring records. You see, Tommy never met a shot he didn't like. It didn't mean he didn't like to mix it up with other big men.

"Tommy and I played against each other in college," Russell once told Comcast Sports Net. Russell played at San Francisco with Jones. "We played in the holiday festival at Madison Square Garden . . . Tommy spent the whole first half telling his teammates not to be afraid. 'To hell with him, to hell with him, to hell with him,' and then Tommy came by and gave me a shot. Well, I gave him one too."

Tommy was tough, but players had to be back then. The game was only a few decades removed from being played in a cage (they used to call basketball players "cagers" once upon a time). He came to Boston and, as part of a newly constructed super-team, the first the league has ever seen, immediately led Boston to the franchise's first championship. In fact, Heinsohn turned in one of the greatest Game 7 performances the league has ever seen.

The Celtics beat the St. Louis Hawks 125–123 in double overtime, and Heinsohn powered the C's with a masterful 37-point, 23-rebound performance. He hit 17 of 33 shots, more than making up for Cousy and Bill Sharman's combined 5-for-40 performances.

It was the first of nine titles Heinsohn won as a player. In fact, he only played one year that didn't end with a championship. Still, he is often overlooked in discussions of great NBA players.

"Tommy as a player and a power forward, he is the most underrated, underappreciated, under-glorified player that I think we've ever had in this league," Bob Cousy told Comcast Sports Net.

There are a lot of reasons that Heinsohn is underappreciated. Part of it is because there are so many other transcendent power forwards in league history while his career came at the beginning of the NBA.

The early '60s were just different. The league was integrated but the best Black players were still on barnstorming teams like the Harlem Globetrotters. Physical fitness meant something different. Players endorsed cigarettes.

Heinsohn was one of the team's biggest smokers. Red Auerbach once told him to quit smoking to get into better shape, but when Heinsohn started gaining weight because of it, Auerbach told him to start smoking again. It's not like Red was innocent. Celtics locker rooms were a thick haze of cigar and cigarette smoke in those days thanks to those two.

Another element of why Heinsohn is overlooked is because he played on a team full of bigger stars. I've already crowned Cousy as an All-Time All-Star starter and, spoiler alert, Bill Russell will be one too. Heinsohn was a six-time All-Star but still not at the top of the team's pecking order.

"When I was a player, I was the whipping boy, because (Red) wasn't going to yell at Cousy or Russell," Heinsohn once said. "If he yelled at Bill Sharman, Sharman might have punched his lights out."

That didn't mean he took a back seat, though. They didn't call him "Tommy gun" for nothing.

He averaged 18 shots per game over his career and more than 20 per game for three seasons, all while averaging less than 30 minutes per game over his career. He led the team in scoring from 1960 to 1962. For a guy being in what might not be optimal cardiovascular condition, Heinsohn loved to run-and-gun, even if some of the gunning was, ahem, ill-advised.

"Sure, he takes a few bad shots now and then," Cousy once told the *Saturday Evening Post* (noted in the book *40 Greatest Players in Boston Celtics Basketball History*), "but over the long haul the confident player is the one who takes the initiative and wins games for you."

One of Heinsohn's biggest contributions to the NBA is also overlooked. He was the president of the NBA's first Player's Association, and he helped organize a near-boycott of the 1964 All-Star Game.

That was the first All-Star Game to be televised, a major milestone in NBA history. The league was still trying to find its footing, and putting the league's biggest stars on TV was a huge step. It was played in Boston, and Heinsohn had the backing of teammates and fellow All-Stars Bill Russell and Sam Jones.

The players were fighting for recognition of their union and benefits to go along with it. As the Boston Garden filled with fans and the television cameras waited, Heinsohn and the players holed themselves up in the locker room. He made sure a security guard was out front with instructions not to let anyone in.

When that guard came in with an ultimatum from Lakers owner Bob Short, Lakers star Elgin Baylor famously responded by saying "You go tell Bob Short to fuck himself."

The owners relented and disaster was avoided. Heinsohn's relationship with the Celtics strained, but it never broke. The players had their union, which is obviously still going strong today.

Heinsohn retired after nine years due to the combination of a foot injury and a burgeoning career in the insurance industry.

I told you life was different back then.

Players often had to take second jobs to make ends meet in those days. Heinsohn got into the insurance business, and it was going really well. The draw of basketball was too great, though, and he was lured back first as part of a broadcasting team with Johnny Most, and then as a coach, which earned him a second induction into the Hall of Fame (he is one of only four men to go in as a player and a coach).

After his coaching days were over, Heinsohn went back into television and has been a fixture there ever since. His green-bleeding bluster has become as entertaining as the basketball over the years, and maybe even more so during some of those lean seasons. Heinsohn could make the Hall a third time for his broadcasting career, and somehow he'd still get overlooked.

"I always loved playing with Tommy Heinsohn because he was a tough guy," Russell said. "Tough guy who doesn't take anything and doesn't give anything. Just does his job."

Heinsohn is the Celtics. But is he an All-Time All-Star?

Kevin Garnett

He'll have to beat out Kevin Garnett, and it's going to be an interesting battle. Kevin Garnett is one of the greatest players of all time, and he was at the forefront of the big-man-as-perimeter-player revolution.

But he only spent six years as a Celtic.

Kevin Garnett was a much better player than Heinsohn over the course of his career, but were his Boston years good enough to eclipse Heinsohn's?

Let's dive into some of the basic raw numbers as a start:

Garnett: 15.7 ppg, 52% FG, 82.7% FT, 8.3 rpg, 2.7 apg

Heinsohn: 18.6 ppg, 40.5% FG, 70% FT, 8.8 rpg, 2 apg

It's already been acknowledged Heinsohn was a bit of a gunner who would occasionally take a bad shot. Heinsohn averaged 18 field goal attempts per game while Garnett averaged 12.5. We also know that Heinsohn played at a time when (a) there was no 3-point shooting, thus lanes were clogged and there wasn't as much space to work and (b) field goal percentages were just bad in general.

So the difference between Garnett's 52 percent and Heinsohn's 40.5 percent isn't quite as wide as it seems. How much better he would have shot in today's game, and vice versa, is hard to quantify.

Still, it's very clearly obvious that Garnett was the better shooter. Garnett's numbers are also depressed a bit by his situation.

He scored 22.4 points per game in his year before joining the Celtics. His All-Star run in Minnesota from 2000 to 2007 was flat-out dominant. He led the NBA in rebounding for four straight years before his trade to Boston, but his numbers tailed off as he willingly took a step back so Ray Allen and Paul Pierce could flourish along with him in Boston.

There's no doubt that Garnett could have put up bigger numbers, but after years of losing in Minnesota, Garnett was driving to win titles in Boston.

Speaking of which, Garnett was only able to win one as a Celtic. Heinsohn has eight.

Of course, we live in a world where Robert Horry has seven. That's not to disparage Horry's career or accomplishments, but

No one talked more than Kevin Garnett on the court, and he used it as a way to dominate a player mentally. He admits, it did backfire on him a couple of times, though. Michael Jordan and Tim Duncan seemed to be immune to his mind games. (KEITH ALLISON VIA WIKIMEDIA COMMONS)

there are obvious flaws to leaning too heavily on titles in this "count da ringzzzzz" culture of ours.

1960s-like dynasties are just not possible nowadays. The system just isn't built for it.

Let's go back to that 1956 draft when Boston got Heinsohn, K. C. Jones, and Russell.

There are no territorial picks anymore, so Boston couldn't leapfrog anyone to take a local star. Also, ownership dynamics (and, frankly, racial attitudes) are radically different nowadays. Boston couldn't use the Ice Capades as incentive like they did in the trade for Russell. Danny Ainge couldn't call David Griffin and say, "Hey, I've got exclusive rights to Taylor Swift concerts, but you guys need to fill the arena on non-basketball nights, so how's about you give us Zion Williamson?"

Even if someone held a gun to Griffin's head and forced him to make that deal, there are salary cap limitations at play that would make it almost impossible to sustain a level of greatness like the '60s Celtics saw.

Remember, Heinsohn quit playing basketball partly because he was doing pretty well in the insurance industry. There's not much that's quite as humbling as winning a championship and thinking you're hot shit but then having to show up for a nine-to-five job the next Monday.

Imagine Steph Curry driving up to your house a week after winning a title so he could assess water damage from a storm.

There is too much money in today's game to maintain the type of rosters that existed in the nine-team NBA of Heinsohn's time. *Nine.*

Today, talent from championship teams is poached as soon as it becomes available. There are few owners who are willing to dive into the luxury tax to keep winners together, but eventually third wheels want to be frontline stars.

So eight titles in nine years is simply a relic of the past. Garnett has one, but it's very easy to see how he could have won three had things gone a little differently.

The 2008-09 Celtics, fresh off their championship, were off to a dominant start. They had whipped off a 19-game winning streak to start the season 27-2. Boston ended up winning 62 games even though Garnett had only played in 57 because of an injured knee.

He couldn't play in the playoffs, and Boston ended up losing in the second round, but there is hardly a soul alive in Boston that won't tell you this Celtics team wasn't better than the championship winner.

"We had a better start in 2009 than we did in 2008," then Celtics coach Doc Rivers told *Sports Illustrated*. "I didn't think anyone could beat us. But Kevin Garnett going down changed everything. Kevin was never the same in 2009 after his injury. He was still good, but he was never the same. Injuries are part of it, but we could have had a real run, and that was taken away."

And then there was 2010, which Boston lost to the, ugh, Los Angeles Lakers. Injuries hurt that team as well, as Kendrick Perkins suffered an ACL tear in Game 6 of the NBA Finals. His replacement, Rasheed Wallace, didn't quite have enough gas in the tank to hold off Pau Gasol. Gasol finished with 18 rebounds, nine offensive. Kobe Bryant had 15 rebounds. They combined for 19 in a fourth quarter the Lakers won by eight.

Three titles would change the calculus of this debate significantly. Three titles, especially consecutively in his first years after arriving, would be comparable to the dynasties of the early NBA days.

So with fairly even statistics but an edge in championships, we have to turn to what Garnett meant to the franchise in his time here. This is his best argument.

Garnett came to Boston after its leanest years.

Boston had never gone more than six years without a title until 1987, but Larry Bird's final title was Boston's last for more than two decades. This is where Rick Pitino happened. This is where all that Paul Pierce drama happened.

This is also where we remind ourselves that we're lucky to love a franchise where 20 years without a title is some cataclysmic event. There are a lot of franchises that would love for their droughts to only be 20 years.

Kevin Garnett came and instantly changed everything.

"When Kevin first got here, he really changed the culture of everything we did around here—from the practice habits to on the court, just the discipline," Paul Pierce said in 2013. "He made everybody accountable, from the ball boys to the chefs to the guy who flew the plane. Everybody was accountable. It was tremendous to just have him around."

No one saw the difference more than Doc Rivers, who often made it clear that the team's new, gritty attitude in the 2007-08 season was directly related to Garnett.

"Kevin made [the transformation] possible," Rivers, who devotes 60 percent to 70 percent of practice time to defense, told *Sports Illustrated*. "When your best player buys in defensively, then everybody has to follow."

It's very important to understand, as much as we can anyway, the intensity with which Garnett played. It's unlike anything you've ever seen, and it's why the world revolved around him.

Garnett set the rules, and he enforced them with the cold ferocity of a medieval king.

He already has a certain energy in his most relaxed state. He is a person who owns rooms simply by entering them.

Then his emotions get involved. They rise higher than yours or mine. Happy Kevin doesn't just smile, he's bouncy, gesturing and laughing. Angry Kevin isn't sullen, he has a stare that could turn Medusa to stone.

So that's his baseline.

On the court he channeled those emotions like Ryu gathering energy for a Hadouken. He found a rage that almost took him to another realm. He reached an intensity that you might see right before a sun explodes into a supernova. If you could plug into him, he could power the Las Vegas Strip.

"You can't teach the beast. It's either in you or it isn't," he once told the great Jackie MacMullan. "You can't just go to the store and buy a six-pack of beast. It don't work like that."

His former teammate Leon Powe can attest to Garnett's intensity. He was on the floor during a practice where Garnett was supposed to take a day off.

"Doc gave him a day off and said 'you don't have to do anything this practice. Just sit over there on the sidelines and let the other guys work,'" Powe said. "We start working, then we look back and we see, like, a shadow just moving up and down the court real fast. And we look back and he was mimicking what we were doing on the court . . . so Doc brought everybody in and said 'everybody go home since KG doesn't want to listen and take a day off.'"

No one can compete with that energy. If someone tried, or if someone couldn't keep up, he was broken.

Take the case of Patrick O'Bryant, a young big man trying to learn his way during Garnett's tenure. Garnett felt he was too passive, so he took it upon himself to teach the young man a thing or two.

The resulting days of constant bombardment were uncomfortable for the rest of the Celtics. Players called the way he berated O'Bryant, the way he'd constantly attack O'Bryant in scrimmages, torture. Doc Rivers called it mean-spirited.

Garnett didn't care.

"I always say, 'I'm not stepping on someone who doesn't want to be stepped on,'" he told MacMullan. "Because this is a no-nonsense league. If you're not in it, and I mean in it today, then they will replace you tomorrow."

The Celtics did just that. They traded O'Bryant away, and his NBA career ended shortly thereafter.

Garnett's mind was his greatest weapon. Doc Rivers's story about an arm wrestling match between Garnett and Glen "Big Baby" Davis on the team plane might sum it up best.

"I thought someone was going to get hurt," said Rivers. "The whole team was in the back of the plane, and I thought Kevin was going to get hurt. 'Big Baby' is huge, and he weighs a hundred more pounds than Kevin. He ran through everyone else in a second, just bam, bam. I knew Kevin would try to win, and I remember telling the coaches, 'I don't like this at all.' I kept saying to the team, 'Hey guys, let's be careful here.'

"If I could get anything on camera, this would be it. It was the most amazing display of will power and mind power. Kevin stared him in the eye and looked at him. He wouldn't stop. You could see 'Baby' go from wanting to win to literally seeing him break down mentally. Kevin made Baby give in. Kevin was just staring at him, saying 'I'm not moving. You're not going to move me.' Then bam, Kevin won."

He left that screaming about being the alpha dog. In some ways, Garnett walked into the Celtics more like a lion taking over a pride, killing cubs to sow his own seed. He was the new king, and everyone fell in line. If a rookie dared eat from the postgame spread before a veteran, the plate was slapped out of his hands. Pregame routines were molded around Garnett's, sometimes in an effort to avoid his pregame rage.

You might think, "wow, KG was a dick."

Yeah, he was at times, but his dickishness was almost a sort of filter to free the team of toxins. Once the squad was set and everyone was on board, Garnett was also an ultimate teammate.

He bought rookies custom suits, because being a professional meant looking like a professional. He put in extra work with younger players who demonstrated a real willingness to learn. When he pushed someone hard in those situations, he was usually just looking for someone that pushed back. Showing fight meant showing strength.

No one benefited more from this kind of tough love than Kendrick Perkins, who was molded from a soft kid who jumped to the NBA from high school into a fierce defensive enforcer who essentially became Garnett's tag team partner on Boston's front line.

"I wanted to make sure that he was worthy. I'm not gonna take anybody that doesn't want to work. I don't like people who complained. I don't like people who don't have a work ethic. I don't do quitters. I wanted to see how he worked on his own," Garnett told *Sports Illustrated* after his retirement. "He was real receptive to it. Then him and I quickly grabbed the chemistry on the court. Perk was just similar to me. We were grinders, kind of physical specimens. Once I got to Boston, in the East Coast, I knew it was gonna be more of a physical game. But he and I communicated and fed off each other really well."

Perkins was the perfect partner for Garnett, who quarterbacked a ferocious Celtics defense with one of the league's highest basketball IQs. He could recognize the offenses opponents were running and guide his teammates to the right spots. He was constantly talking, sometimes even to himself. With Perkins behind him, Garnett could be even more aggressive, which just heightened the entire defensive experience.

Offensively, Garnett was unselfish almost to a fault. His nickname could have been "shoot that," because it's probably what Celtics fans yelled at Garnett more than anything. When he did decide it was his time to shine, he could still bring it with the best of them.

He averaged 18 points and 13 rebounds in the 2008 NBA Finals, including a 24-point, 13-rebound Game 1 and a 26-point, 14-rebound Game 6. He scored 20 or more in 13 games in that playoff run and shot better than 50 percent in 14. Overall Garnett finished his Boston career averaging just under a double-double in the playoffs with 17.5 points and 9.9 rebounds per game.

So where does this leave us with Heinsohn?

He scored a little bit more than Garnett did, even in the playoffs (he averaged 19.8 ppg in the playoffs). He definitely had more playoff success, which matters some, but also not quite as much as it would had situations been different.

I don't want to be the latest in a line of people who overlook Heinsohn and his impact on this team. In fact, I would argue that no single person besides Red Auerbach has meant more to the franchise. He won as a player and a coach and made the Hall of Fame for both. He's a beloved broadcaster who could make the Hall for that as well. Heinsohn has been a lifelong Celtic whose accomplishments are truly underappreciated.

Sigh. Now I have to say this.

I have to go with Garnett. There's one thing I can't get past when it comes to this debate. Heinsohn, for all his greatness, was more of a complementary player whereas Garnett was the culture-changer.

Garnett only being in Boston for six years makes this a tough debate. Garnett coming away from his run with just one ring makes this a tough debate.

But Garnett's indescribable influence on this team is too much to ignore. The way he took a team at its lowest point and almost single-handedly rekindled Boston's championship spirit is too great of an accomplishment.

Garnett edges out Heinsohn for a spot on this All-Time All-Star team. If he'd won those other two titles, he might even have challenged the current, unquestioned starter on this team.

KEVIN McHALE

I should say that I wouldn't even be writing this book if it wasn't for Kevin McHale. When I was a young, terrible basketball player in the early 1980s, I was told to study McHale's post moves. Eventually, I got good enough at them to carry this basketball thing into a career playing the game and writing about it.

And those moves, boy, they were something.

They say necessity is the mother of invention, and back in the old days, finding a way to score in a very crowded lane required a whole lot of ingenuity. Coming up with the types of moves McHale developed required him to be part choreographer, part dancer, and part strategist. McHale was as much an artist as he was a basketball player.

The first step in post scoring requires feeling how you're being defended. This is a back-to-the-basket endeavor, which puts a player in a unique position; you don't see your defender, and you purposely get as close to him as possible.

It might seem counterintuitive, but the close proximity is necessary to understand where your first move is going to be. Is he more on your right hip? Then you lean into that, put your left hand up as a target, and hope to hell the ball gets to you quickly enough to take advantage of it.

Strategy kicks in from there. What shot is available? How often can you get to that shot? When is the right time to fake that shot and then go to something else? Where is the help defense coming from? When should you pass to keep that help defense honest?

The only way to make this whole thing work is to have the footwork to dance through all the trees around the rim. Knowing how to jump and catch, establish a pivot foot, power dribble into someone's body, then fake and spin yourself to freedom is quite the skill, and McHale had it all.

McHale rises up for a jump hook. Notice the Pistons defenders on the floor and not challenging him. That's probably because they just bit on a fake and were expecting something else. (STEVE LIPOFSKY WWW.BASKET-BALLPHOTO.COM)

"It got to a point where we were calling Kevin McHale 'The Man of a Thousand Moves,'" Atlanta Hawks legend and Celtics rival Dominique Wilkins once said on NBA TV. "You could not guard him one-on-one on the box. He had such great footwork. He did a great job of feeling the contact. Once he felt you, you were done."

McHale's signature move was the "up-and-under," where he'd fake a shot, and while the defender was in the air (because they almost always bit on the fake), he'd quickly pivot and duck under him to score. The 6'10" McHale would use his eight-foot wingspan to sell the fake, putting the ball right in front of a defender's face, and then use his reach to snake under him to score.

The move was deadly, mostly because defenders had no choice but to respect his ability to make those short jumpers or jump hooks. If they backed off he could just turn and shoot. If they tried to cut his path to the lane, he'd just power dribble and drop step his way to a layup.

"I played a lot of one-on-one growing up, and I didn't grow until late," McHale once told Garnett on his show, *Area 21*. "I was small, so I had to learn how to get shots over people that were bigger than me. I played against guys that were older, and taller than me, and stronger than me, and better than me. So I had to be tricky."

He is one of the greatest post players ever. We can fight about whether Hakeem Olajuwon was better (that debate could fill a book of its own).

And the Celtics basically stole him.

There are three trades that define the Boston Celtics front office legacy of swindling their rivals.

The first got them Bill Russell (which I mentioned earlier and we'll get to—woo, boy, that's a doozy). The third, which I also mentioned, is the Pierce and Garnett trade with Brooklyn where the return is still being realized. The second one created the Big 3 of the '80s.

In June of 1980, the Celtics traded the first and 13th pick of the NBA Draft to the Golden State Warriors for Robert Parish and the third pick. The Warriors wanted Joe Barry Carroll, and they knew the Utah Jazz did as well. At the same time, Robert Parish wasn't working out, and Carroll was going to replace him.

Also at the same time, McHale was a star at Minnesota, and the Celtics were enamored with him. There was talk that he'd have been their pick if they couldn't make a trade, but the Warriors bit.

They took Carroll. The Jazz took Darrell Griffith. The Celtics took McHale.

As a side note, Carroll's nickname might have been "Joe Barely Cares," but he actually spent 10 years in the league and averaged 17.7 points, 7.7 rebounds, and 1.8 assists per game. McHale averaged 17.9/7.3/1.7 over 13 years. The entirety of the trade was a heist for the Celtics, but Carroll wasn't some bust that sucked. He had a productive career. Who knows what would have happened if their roles were switched?

What we do know is that McHale immediately came in and helped the Celtics win a title in his rookie year. He spent the first five years of his career mostly coming off the bench, carrying on the strong Celtics tradition of Frank Ramsey and John Havlicek as a starter-level player in a reserve role. McHale won the Sixth Man of the Year twice in a row, the first person to ever accomplish that. He became an All-Star and made the All-Defensive team in that role.

Once he became a starter, the Boston Celtics had their Big 3. The Celtics traded away Cedric Maxwell, and McHale responded by making six straight All-Star Games and averaging 20-plus points per game over the first five of those seasons. He twice led the NBA in field goal percentage, and is currently the third most accurate scorer in Celtics history. He used his ridiculous wingspan to block more than two shots per game during his peak.

Though, at least one of those blocks came as a joke.

"Kevin McHale, one time, did one of the dirtiest things anybody can do to an opposing player," Bird once told ESPN. "He told his buddy, a college friend, a teammate (at one point) at the end of the game in Golden State we were up pretty big—and we were just getting ready to go out of the game—and Kevin told him when he came in, he said, 'When you get the ball in the low post, you just turn and shoot it over me, and I'll just act like I'm defending you.' Sure enough, they threw it in there, he turned and Kevin batted the shot about six rows up into the stands. And I mean I felt so bad for the guy, and the guy was pissed. And I went over to (Celtics coach) K. C. Jones and I said, 'Get me out of here. This kid's out of control, this kid's out of control.' It was the worst thing I'd ever seen on the basketball court, but that's why I remember it to this day. You don't do that to your friend (laughs)."

This was McHale's personality. While dragging Bird to a commercial shoot drove his agent nuts sometimes, McHale was more than willing to have fun with moments. He appeared on

There's a chance Dennis Johnson is saying "Kevin says to tell Larry . . ." here. They played great together on the floor, but McHale was a little too happy-go-lucky for the serious Bird. (STEVE LIPOFSKY WWW.BASKETBALL PHOTO.COM)

the hit TV show *Cheers* twice. The difference between Bird and McHale caused some tension

"Larry would always come to me and say, 'Hey, go tell Kevin this,' and Kevin would come to me and say, 'Go tell Larry that,'" Danny Ainge told Boston.com. "They were such great players, but sometimes they didn't know how to talk to each other and how to yell at each other. But they knew how to yell at me."

McHale acknowledges some butting of heads, but he says it never got in the way of getting the job done on the court.

"I remember after a game in Atlanta once, Larry looks at me, we're having a beer, and he looks at me and says, 'Can you believe they pay us to do this?,'" McHale once told Boston.com. "I started laughing and said, 'They pay us. Plus we get free beer, which is a good deal.' That's how I felt about my entire career. I rode my bike to the gym every single day as a kid to play, and now they're paying me to do something I went out of the way to do every single day of my life. I was always like, 'That's unbelievable.'"

Just a couple of buds, kicking back, crushing brews . . . and the '80s Pistons.

They grew up differently, so they were different people. For example, Bird is one of the best passers in NBA history. McHale was nicknamed the "black hole," and his best passing season netted him 2.7 assists per game.

So what if he mostly only passed because he had to. His job wasn't as a playmaker. His job was to put the ball in the basket. He did it best against Detroit on March 3, 1985, when he dropped 56 points on 20-for-28 shooting. He also shot 12-for-13 from the free throw line, had 16 rebounds (10 offensive), 3 blocks, a steal, and . . . hey whaddya know! *Four* assists!

"The only time I ever scored that many points before was in a pickup game when I was 12. And then we played almost five hours," McHale told Boston.com in 2017.

Said Bird in that same article, "Once you realize what's happening . . . you know, you don't get there very often, where you have a chance to do something like that. When you get there, you defer even more. You get the guy the ball. That's what I tried to do with Kevin. You defer a lot when someone gets hot anyway."

McHale took himself out of the game, much to Bird's chagrin. He was all about embarrassing those Pistons teams whenever he could, and this opportunity to pile on a few extra jabs felt wasted.

Of course, by now you know this was the game Bird used as motivation to score his 60 less than two weeks later.

This game was actually, essentially, where the Big 3 was born. Cedric Maxwell was hurt on the bench at the time and he saw his young backup piling up buckets, many of which were assisted by Bird, who thought Maxwell wasn't exactly working hard to come back.

Max was traded that offseason, but while that issue with the Celtics roster was resolved, a new threat had surfaced for McHale and the Celtics.

He fought through a sore Achilles in their 1986 championship. In 1987, he played through what was essentially a broken foot. He'd use a patio chair as a walker around his hotel, then somehow find a way to play in the NBA Finals at night. And oh, by the way, he averaged 20.5 points and nine rebounds per game while doing it.

He had surgery on his right foot that offseason, and hasn't walked normally since.

That 1986-87 season was McHale's best. Foot and ankle issues would flare up for the rest of his career, and happen more frequently as he got older. He compensated by occasionally stepping out to the 3-point line.

I wouldn't necessarily call him the league's first stretch-four, but he showed a pretty good ability to take his face-up game past the arc. He hit 23 of 69 3-pointers (33.3 percent) in 1989-90 and 15 of 37 (40.5 percent) in 1990-91.

By then he was back on the bench. He limped into the sunset in 1993.

There are people in this book who defy the current "load management" efforts in the NBA. There have been a few guys in NBA history that can handle unreal workloads. It's sort of like that smoker who dies at 90-something-years-old without any real health issues. It happens.

McHale, though, might be the poster boy for it. In today's NBA, McHale would have missed more games when his foot issues first cropped up, and he surely wouldn't have been allowed to play on a broken foot. It's tough to say how he would have done with that kind of focus on his health and something other than a "rub some dirt on it" attitude.

It's sort of pointless to even speculate about it, but I'm doing it anyway because I wanted more. I still do.

It's a shame post play has been so minimized in today's NBA. I understand that the numbers just make it an inefficient shot, but maybe if there was some more Kevin McHale in these players, shots would be easier to make.

The pendulum is always swinging in sports. Dominant point guards demand space, so big men can't spend too much time clogging the lane. They have been taught how to shoot, and their ability to space the floor means the Kemba Walkers of the world can knife their way through the paint and do their thing.

They have not been taught the intricate dance that is life in the post. They have not learned the footwork that it takes to spin defenders into oblivion.

Of course, it's not easy to learn, and not everyone has the ability to pull it off, even if they tried to learn it.

Kevin McHale had it. He arguably did it as well or better than anyone else to pick up a basketball. He might not just be the best power forward in Celtics history; he might be the best in NBA history.

Final Verdict:
Starter: Kevin McHale
Backup: Kevin Garnett

CENTER

The Candidates

Dave Cowens
Robert Parish
Bill Russell

No position in basketball has changed quite as much as center. Al Horford, who spent three seasons with the Boston Celtics, might be the perfect encapsulation of that evolution.

He took 12 3-pointers over his first five regular seasons and 65 over his first eight. Then, during the 2015-16 regular season, he took 256.

He took 671 as a Celtic.

That's not how it used to be.

The classic center archetype is a 7-foot-tall behemoth who sets picks, blocks shots, rebounds, and scores when he gets the ball in the post. The golden age of big men included legends like Hakeem Olajuwon, Patrick Ewing, David Robinson, and Shaquille O'Neal. Shaq was really the last of the true dominant centers as the game has evolved to clearing out of the paint to provide as much space for slashers and cutters as possible.

Joel Embiid is a bit of a throwback, but he's not shy about launching 3s, which just goes to show how things have changed.

The Celtics haven't had a truly great center in a long time, but they've had a few of the best to ever do it.

Sooooooo ... we all cool with putting Bill Russell in?

Any objections?

Going once?

Going twice?

You better believe there's a celebration of Russell coming. We are making sure we give this man his proper due.

In the meantime, Dave Cowens versus Robert Parish is a tough debate. Parish has a bit more longevity but not the list of accolades that Cowens had. Parish also played in an era when dominant big men were the norm, and making something like the All-NBA team meant beating out fellow Hall of Famers Moses Malone, Patrick Ewing, Kareem Abdul-Jabbar, Hakeem Olajuwon, Ralph Sampson, and Jack Sikma.

That's not to say Cowens's competition was weak. He had to contend with Wes Unseld, Bob Lanier, Elvin Hayes, and even a few years of the end of Wilt Chamberlain's career (oh, and *also* Kareem, because Kareem played forever and was a beast the whole time). Parish and Cowens even had to face each other for four seasons.

That's heavy lifting for a 6'9" center.

Cowens wasn't just some small guy trying to play a big man's game. He was a supreme athlete who could run the floor, sky for boards, and finish with touch. If Tommy Heinsohn, his coach for seven full seasons, could have crafted a perfect small-ball center for his run-and-gun style of play, Cowens might have been the result.

I mention games that could translate into today's NBA and Cowens might be a good candidate. The 3-pointer became part of the NBA later in his career, and Cowens tested his touch by stepping out occasionally, but not often enough to say for sure whether he could have become a stretch big. However, everything else in his game works because Coach Heinsohn's style of play would have worked.

He dropped a 25-point, 21-rebound, 10-assist triple-double in Game 1 of the 1976 NBA Finals. That was the series with the greatest game ever played. That's the one where I've already talked about the amazing performances by Jo Jo White and John Havlicek, both of whom have already made this team. Well, Cowens was also good in that game, playing 55 minutes and finishing with 26 points and 19 rebounds. He averaged 20.5 points and 16.3 rebounds in that series.

Parish never put up those kinds of numbers, but he also had Kevin McHale and Larry Bird getting boards in a little bit slower game. Cowens's 1973 Celtics put up 8,511 shots, 1,214 more than Parish's 1985 Celtics, for example. Heinsohn had them running around and pushing the pace, so there were a few extra boards per game for him to get. Cowens also played 39 minutes per game while Parish played 31.

Uh oh, you know what this means right?

The differences in eras? The disparity between opportunities?

We need an equalizer. We need ... *analytics!*

For those of you still holding this book rather than throwing it into a fire, let's just calm down. We're not doing stupidly deep dives with plot lines on an X and Y axis. We're just going to look at a couple of things by evening out the numbers a bit.

Here is how they compare as Celtics per 100 possessions:

Cowens: 20.6 points, 15.2 rebounds, 4.8 assists, 1.4 steals, 1.1 blocks, 1.2 turnovers

Parish: 25.2 points, 15.3 rebounds, 2.3 assists, 1.2 steals, 2.4 blocks, 3.3 turnovers

Well, that looks a bit different, doesn't it? Parish certainly benefits here, which is no surprise because he played less. Let's look at some of the advanced percentages to help get a closer look:

Cowens: .496 true shooting, 17.1 total rebound percentage, 13.7 assist percentage, 1.3 block percentage, 17.2 Player Efficiency Rating

Parish: .587 true shooting, 17.7 total rebound percentage, 6.9 assist percentage, 2.8 block percentage, 19.8 Player Efficiency Rating

Parish was the better shooter but he took some higher percentage shots. He was a better offensive rebounder (11.5 OReb percentage vs. 8.1 OReb percentage), which gave him better advanced rebound numbers even though Cowens had some staggering raw numbers. Ultimately, even with the total numbers Cowens put up, Parish grabbed a higher percentage of the available rebounds when he played.

Cowens was the better passer, setting up teammates nearly twice as often as Parish. If there's anything that highlights the dichotomy of their roles, this stat is it. Back in Chief's days (he got the Chief nickname because he was silent and stoic like the character in *One Flew Over the Cuckoo's Nest*), he could face up and drill an 18-footer. Back then, that was spreading the floor.

In the mid-'80s, it looked like both teams were square dancing with each other in the middle of the lane, so 18 feet actually provided a sliver of daylight that could be attacked. That wasn't his preferred zone, mind you. He was much more comfortable do-si-do'ing his way through the lane to finish off Larry Bird assists.

Cowens was a small-ball center who was asked to move the ball and then himself to put pressure on the defense and create exploitable cracks.

"When Cowens was drafted, Boston media members were skeptical that someone 6-foot-8 could match up with the 7-foot centers who dominated that era," said Celtics historian and blogger Mike Dynon. "But Cowens was quick and mobile, with a soft shooting touch. Coach Tommy Heinsohn recognized the rookie could be the perfect center for the Celtics' fast-breaking, up-tempo offense—what today would be known as "small ball." In the low post, Cowens possessed an effective jump hook, and he could also turn and shoot with good range from the high post. His trademark became the 18-foot jump shot as a trailer on the fast break."

Cowens won two titles with Boston while Parish won three. Cowens has the accolades edge on Parish though.

He was an MVP in 1973. The best Parish has ever finished is fourth in MVP voting. Cowens was a co–Rookie of the Year. He was a three-time All-NBA player to Parish's two. He made three All-Defensive teams, something Parish never did.

Awards do favor Cowens, but, again, Parish had absolute giants of the game ahead of him at his position, which hurt him come award time. It certainly skews things toward Cowens, but it feels like some of the better performance numbers belong to Parish.

This is still a tough call, so let's dive more into their histories to see what they meant to the franchise as a whole.

DAVE COWENS

"The NBA of the '70s was extremely physical, which was perfect for Cowens' game and personality," Dynon said. "He also didn't put up with much from anyone, which led to the infamous Mike Newlin incident. Newlin was a guard with the Rockets, and one night in Boston he flopped on a Cowens drive. Offensive foul. Cowens argued and got nowhere so, enraged, he took a running start, sent Newlin flying with a body-block, and screamed at the ref, 'Now that's a foul!'"

And so begins our story of Cowens's bad-assery.

Tommy Heinsohn was Cowens's coach with the Celtics, but NBA life then wasn't quite like it is today. We've got high-light shows and countless media outlets that thrust a college prospect into the national conversation.

Heinsohn, though, didn't know much about Cowens until he got around to seeing him play.

"I immediately said, 'Wow, this guy is a bundle of energy and ferocity.' So, we used that on the fast break," Heinsohn said. The Celtics would go on to use Cowens like many small-ball centers are used in the modern game: moving away from the basket and becoming a playmaker. "He had the ball, and he would make Wilt come out, and it was a style that became very, very successful for us."

There was only one way for the 6'9" Cowens to play, and that was all out, all the time. Maybe that explains why he burned himself out six years into his career.

"Dave's most outstanding trait was his desire," Heinsohn once said in an *Investors* magazine interview. "When he put his mind to something, 100% of him went with it. He could be a ferocious player. He was a very competitive person."

Cowens was a workhorse and a monster rebounder, but unfortunately for him even his 16 rebounds per game in 1976 are nowhere near the top of Boston's all-time list, because Bill Russell never averaged fewer than 18.6 in 12 years. (ROBERT KINGSBURY, *SPORTING NEWS*, VIA WIKIMEDIA COMMONS)

His former teammate Paul Silas said, "I thought he was a wild man. I'd never seen anybody with that much talent play that aggressively."

Cowens immediately made an impact with that combination, attacking players bigger than him and coming out on top. He was one of the league's best rebounders and most intense defenders. Players around the league took notice, voting him Most Valuable Player in his second season (players voted on the award back then).

In his third season, he became a champion.

"Words to describe Dave Cowens: intense, relentless, tenacious. Those qualities were on display in the most iconic play of his career, during Game 6 of the 1974 Finals versus Milwaukee," Dynon said. "With the score tied in the final minute of regulation, the Celtics were desperate for a stop. On defense, Cowens switched onto guard Oscar Robertson, one of the best ballhandlers and shooters in NBA history. But Cowens poked away the Big O's dribble, scrambled after the loose ball, and dove on it as he skidded across the court while the shot clock ran out on the Bucks."

He became a champion again two years later, but things changed after the 1976 title. The Celtics traded Silas away, which contributed to Cowens losing his lust for the game. For a guy who played with unrelenting passion, losing this meant losing an edge.

One of the legends from this point in the Dave Cowens story is that time he drove a cab. As the story is sometimes told, Cowens took a break from basketball so he could drive a taxi for a living. He did take a personal leave for a couple of months, and he did take odd jobs where he helped sell pine trees and run a racetrack. He also did, in fact, drive a cab, but it wasn't exactly the way the legend tells it. Here's how he explained it to the Huffington Post.

"I think that was in '77. We were in the playoffs. A buddy of mine from Kentucky was in town, and I said, 'Hey, let's go get a cab.' At that time, for like $35, you could get a cab to drive. You had to pay for your own gas, but whatever you made you could keep for yourself.

"We were driving around, trying to pick people up. But no one wanted to get in the cab because there were two of us in the front seat.

"So I let my buddy out and then business picked up. And then a crazy thing happened. I was stopped at an intersection, at Boylston and Tremont. A guy gets in and asks me to take him to Newton. As we're driving down to the Mass Pike, he tells me he's a reporter. He had been covering a Bruins game that night when he heard that Cowens was driving a cab. So he left the hockey game and started walking the streets of Boston, looking for my cab, and he found it at that intersection. Now you tell me, what are the odds of that happening?

"He wrote a story about it, and eventually—because not too long before that I had taken my leave of absence—people started thinking that I had quit basketball to drive a cab. I drove the cab for one night, just as a lark, just for something to do."

A leave of absence seems hard to comprehend. Cowens felt burned out by the grind of the NBA and had to be coaxed a bit to return by Red Auerbach, who thought his work at a racetrack was both inappropriate and, very likely, a violation of the contract he was still under.

Cowens came back as a player-coach, and was an All-Star in that and two more seasons before suddenly hanging it up in 1980, after Larry Bird's rookie season. The burden of coaching and playing was just too much for Cowens to handle. To top things off, the team was losing.

However, after two years off, he wanted to come back, and the Milwaukee Bucks, then coached by Cowens's former Celtics teammate Don Nelson, were willing to give him a shot. They traded Quinn Buckner for him, but it didn't work out. The Cowens experience in Milwaukee was a failure. Buckner gave the Celtics some production off the bench, mostly on defense, and he won a title as part of the 1984 team.

Cowens was finished, but he left a lasting memory of a nonstop grinder with a ton of talent to back it up.

"I was very much a Dennis the Menace on the court," he said. "My attitude was to play all out, and to just let it rip. I was always running. I stayed in constant motion, running fast and trying to wear my opponent down."

ROBERT PARISH

Parish was the eighth pick in the 1976 NBA Draft by the Golden State Warriors, but things weren't exactly going well there. Their record got worse each year he was there and they made the playoffs just once. In 1980, the Warriors were ready to move on from their underwhelming center and they jumped at the chance to jump to the first pick by swapping with Boston while unloading Parish.

"Once I hung up with the Golden State Warriors when they told me I was traded to the Boston Celtics, I cheered," Parish once said on the Locked on Celtics podcast. "I jumped up

Parish was so good, he could score on Detroit's Bill Laimbeer and read his palm at the same time. Parish averaged 17.1 points, 9.6 rebounds, 1.8 assists, and 54.4 percent from the field in 63 games against Laimbeer. Parish was 40-23 in those matchups. (STEVE LIPOFSKY WWW .BASKETBALLPHOTO.COM)

and down. I treated myself to a stiff drink, because I went from purgatory to the penthouse. . . . For me and my career, being traded to the Celtics changed the trajectory of my career."

Said former teammate Artis Gilmore, "I thought Robert was one of the most extraordinary players ever. I remember the trade that sent him from Golden State to the Boston Celtics, and right from the beginning he seemed to be a perfect fit for that organization. It really turned his whole career around."

Parish arrived as Cowens was retiring and Bird was going into his second year. Going to the Celtics didn't just give him more opportunity to play with better players, it rekindled a love for the game. It's odd to say that the guy who played in more games than anyone else in NBA history was ready to quit, but life with the Warriors might have driven him to it.

"It gave me incentive and I was motivated to play the game again," Parish said. "I was seriously thinking about having a very short basketball career before the trade because of all the losing that I experienced with the Warriors and getting blamed for the Warriors demise."

Life was much better in Boston, where his arrival with Kevin McHale created perhaps the greatest frontline in NBA history. At the height of their powers, the Celtics Big 3 was as dominant as any trio. With Bird's passing, McHale's post moves, and Parish being able to slide into that in-between spot as needed to launch his rainbow jumper, the Celtics felt unstoppable.

"It was a beautiful time in my professional career, playing with like-minded people," Parish said of his time in Boston. "We're all on the same page, competing for one goal and that's to achieve excellence in regards to the NBA championship. I have so much respect for that team because everybody on that team put their egos aside for that team. And that's rare. You're talking about some major egos in that locker room and we sacrificed our egos to try to achieve a common goal and that's why I have so much respect for those players."

Parish kept himself in shape by practicing martial arts. Bill Laimbeer learned that the hard way in 1987 in a game that, fortunately for Parish, became famous for something entirely different.

In the second quarter of Game 5 of the Eastern Conference Semifinals, Laimbeer moved into position to "box out" Robert Parish, a move that included a left elbow to Parish's throat. Parish responded with a four-hammer combination to Laimbeer's head and face.

Parish wouldn't even be called for a foul, though he did get suspended for Game 6. Later in the game, Bird stole the ball, reducing Parish's reaction to the hated Pistons and their dirty tactics to a footnote for the game.

"I think hate is a strong word," Parish said. "But it was a healthy dislike."

As further proof that Parish, though generally quiet, was no pushover, here's his account of a showdown with the notoriously ornery Michael Jordan as a member of the Chicago Bulls.

"Michael had the tendency to test his teammates, especially the new faces on the team," Parish said. "I think it was more of a test than a threat. He was just testing my reaction to his being a bully, and I didn't back down. He said he would kick my butt, and I told him if he felt that strongly about it, come and get some. And that was the end of it. We didn't have another confrontation."

Parish was probably just as much of a badass as Cowens, but he didn't wear his heart on his sleeve quite like Big Red did. If there's one thing that really separated them, it was the intensity with which Cowens played versus Parish's quiet, systematic professionalism.

This may be the toughest of all the choices in assembling this team. Both are very deserving. However, there are a couple of things that break this tie for me.

The advanced numbers even the production out. One of Cowens's biggest advantages in this debate is an edge in the raw counting stats. Evening them out to 100 possessions to account for Parish's fewer minutes per game changes that dynamic. Statistically, Parish is the better player during the time he spent on the floor.

Is it fair to compare Cowens's situation and attitude to what Parish faced? Maybe not entirely, but it's the best way to compare the two as directly as possible.

Parish also played 14 seasons for the Celtics compared to 10 for Cowens, and Cowens was so burned out by 1976 that he needed to take two months off. Parish played 1,106 games for the Celtics, second only to John Havlicek. Cowens played in 726, nearly 400 fewer than Parish. That matters. Parish also played 184 playoff games to Cowens's 89.

Parish is still the team's career leader in defensive rebounds and offensive rebounds (though they didn't differentiate in Bill Russell's day, which is why Russell is the team's all-time leading rebounder and Parish is second). He's fourth in team history in made field goals. He's first in blocks.

The deeper you dive into things, the more Parish pulls away. Cowens probably had a few better individual seasons, and it seems unfathomable that an MVP doesn't get in at his position over a non-MVP. Part of that is my belief that, had they switched places, Parish could have been the MVP. After all, he did finish fourth in the vote one season with a much more loaded field ahead of him.

It's fair to say both aren't fully appreciated. Cowens played in the NBA's lost era. Basketball in the 1970s was full of upheaval, a drug problem, and a battle for the league's very survival. Parish played next to one of the top two players in team history and one of the best power forwards to ever play the game. He also played in the NBA's golden era of centers, so there are myriad reasons he was overshadowed.

This shouldn't be like that Seinfeld joke about the Three Tenors: Placido Domingo, Luciano Pavarotti, and . . . that other guy. There's a reason José Carreras was on stage with those giants just like there's a reason why Parish was part of a championship core with the Celtics. It's because he's a legend on his own. And he's on this All-Time All-Star team.

BILL RUSSELL

That brings us to Mr. William Fenton Russell.

You know him as Bill. Sometimes people call him Russ, or "the greatest winner of all time." I think he also goes by "baddest man on the planet."

In 2017, Bill Russell stood on stage in New York City to accept a lifetime achievement award from the NBA. Joining him on the stage were some of basketball's greatest centers of all time.

Alonzo Mourning. Shaquille O'Neal. David Robinson. Dikembe Mutombo. Kareem Abdul-Jabbar.

He stood there and took it all in. For a full five seconds he looked at this amazing array of big men through the years, standing there to honor him. It felt poignant. It felt emotional.

Russell then pointed to each of them, put his left hand up to his mouth, and said, "I would kick your ass."

The place exploded. Russell let out his usual shriek of a laugh. It was glorious.

Oh, and he was right. He would. He'd find a way. He always did.

Let's begin with Mr. Russell's resume, which is quite impressive.

He is a five-time MVP. *Five*. Not only that, he finished second twice, third twice, and fourth twice. He's an 11-time All-NBA player and a 12-time All-Star over his 13-year career. He won 11 titles, suffering the indignance of failing to win it all only twice.

He averaged 15 points and 22.5 rebounds per game. He averaged 16.2 points and 24.9 rebounds per game in the playoffs. He played in 10 Game 7s and never lost a single one.

Bill Russell also didn't average a single block over his career ... because they didn't count blocks back then. How many did he actually block? There are some people that think it was somewhere around six shots per game. Some think it was close to eight or maybe even 10. You can do a YouTube search and see footage of him actually doing it. Considering the way guys shot the ball in his day, it's not impossible to think he'd have a ton of chances at blocked shots.

He was the first African American to become an NBA head coach, which he did while he was still playing for the Celtics.

Russell was the NBA's first Black superstar.

Red Auerbach and Bill Russell forged an early bond based on respect, something Russell never thought he would find in a coach. That mutual respect was perhaps the biggest reason why "Celtics Pride" exists today. (THE *SPORTING NEWS* ARCHIVE VIA WIKIMEDIA COMMONS)

The NBA had been integrated in 1950, six years before Russell joined the league. Chuck Cooper was the first Black player drafted by an NBA team, taken by the Celtics but gone before Russell got there. But the arrival of Black players didn't mean the floodgates opened for them.

Some of the best of the time played for the Harlem Globetrotters. In fact, it was the Globetrotters' wins over the champion Minneapolis Lakers in a pair of exhibitions that helped pave the way for NBA integration.

If it wasn't for a bad contract negotiation, Russell might have been on the Globetrotters too. But when that went south, Russell entered the 1956 NBA Draft.

Now here's where the Ice Capades come in.

The Rochester Royals had the first pick in the draft (Tommy Heinsohn had already been taken by Boston with the territorial pick). They were struggling to turn a profit and the arena needed to be filled when basketball wasn't being played. Red Auerbach and Walter Brown, the Celtics owner and one of the founders of the Ice Capades, knew this was the case and went to the Royals with a proposition.

You don't draft Bill Russell, and we'll throw you the ice show for a bit to help pump a few bucks into your operation.

They bit, and the Celtics were in business. For the record, it didn't work out for the Royals. They moved to Cincinnati in 1957, then to Kansas City, and then to Sacramento where they now exist as the Sacramento Kings. So, let's just say their current reputation of poor front office moves is rooted in team history and is a long-standing tradition.

The St. Louis Hawks had the second pick, but they moved it to Boston for St. Louis native and local hero Ed Macauley and Cliff Hagan. Macauley had actually asked to be traded to St. Louis to be closer to his family.

The Celtics beat the Hawks for a championship in Russell's first season but lost to them in his second, partly because Russell was hurt. Then Boston won eight championships in a row.

So the Hawks can say, "Hey, we got a title out of that trade!" which is nice for them because that was their only one. The Hawks lost to Boston twice more in that run, the last being

1961, which was the franchise's last trip to the Finals. They are now the Atlanta Hawks.

You get the picture. Russell and the '60s Celtics laid waste to the league. This is what he got future Hall of Famer Dolph Schayes to say after a single playoff game against him: "How much does that guy make a year? It would be to our advantage if we paid him off for five years to get away from us in the rest of this series."

Minneapolis coach John Kundla said, in that same piece, "We don't fear the Celtics without Bill Russell. Take him out and we can beat them. . . . He's the guy who whipped us psychologically. Russell has our club worrying every second. Every one of the five men is thinking Russell is covering him on every play. He blocks a shot, and before you know it, Boston is getting a basket, and a play by Russell has done it."

The psychological warfare was Russell's secret weapon, maybe because he was constantly engaged in it outside of basketball. The rampant racism of his time was constant at home and on the road. Throughout his life, he witnessed it over and over again, and when it robbed him of accolades he earned on the court, he steeled himself against the slight by doing something no bigot could take from him.

Win.

His ability to focus was arguably his greatest strength. Drowning out the outside noise gave him a singular focus on the court, and he used it to learn every player's tendencies. He applied it by baiting players into thinking they could use a move against him and, when they went back to it for a second, third, or fourth time, he'd feed them what reporters used to call a Wilson burger (Wilson made the basketballs back then, and the blocks were like feeding the player . . . you get it). Once players were blocked, often seemingly out of nowhere, they'd nervously look for him the next time they felt like they were in a position to score.

Russell didn't have the benefit of an on/off switch like someone like Kevin Garnett. Normal KG is amiable and willing to talk and have fun, but he whipped himself into heated frenzies on the court to get himself to his desired competitive level. Russell had to be on alert at all times.

He grew up in the segregated South, and experienced some of the worst a racist world had to offer. His ascension to NBA stardom did little to cut the edge off some of the overt racism.

Black players were refused service at a Lexington, Kentucky, restaurant before an exhibition game.

"All of the black players were denied service—not just the black players for the Celtics," Russell's teammate Satch Sanders said.

Once their hotel realized the men were members of the NBA, they changed their tune, but that was no consolation to them. They wanted to be treated as equals simply because they were equal, not because they could play basketball.

Hotel management told them they'd be denied service if they weren't NBA players.

"Based on this criteria, Bill Russell quickly decided that he would not play in the game," Sanders said. "The other black players on the Celtics—myself, Sam Jones, K. C. Jones—felt the same way about the situation. It was an easy decision to make."

Russell and the Black players left. The white players played.

Someone broke into his Boston home in 1963, vandalizing it with racist graffiti and defecating in his bed. Boston's reputation in racial matters has never been great, and this was a time in history when that reputation was earned.

"He had issues with the Boston scene," Sanders told the *Boston Globe*. "And those had never, in his mind, been cleared up."

"Boston itself was a flea market of racism," Russell wrote in his memoir *Second Wind*. "It had all varieties, old and new, and in their most virulent form. The city had corrupt, city hall-crony racists, brick-throwing, send-'em-back-to-Africa racists, and in the university areas phony radical-chic racists. . . . Other than that, I liked the city."

All the while, Russell channeled his rage toward two things: social justice and winning basketball games. He wanted to use his fame and fortune to fight for things he stood for no matter how it impacted him personally. Whether it was standing by Muhammad Ali's fight against the Vietnam War or attending the March on Washington, Russell was very visible with other star Black athletes of his day.

By winning basketball games, Russell made sure no one, no matter how bigoted, could refute a Black player's greatness. Racist attitudes during the beginning of his career created a feeling that Black players weren't smart or coordinated enough to play a sophisticated sport like basketball; that they were not human enough to embrace its intricacies and were, instead, better suited for more "primitive" activities like running fast and jumping high.

Russell could do those things, too, but he used all the tools at his disposal to meet his goals. His mind games were bolstered by his elite athleticism. He was a world-class high-jumper, and he was ready to compete in that event in the Olympics. There was a plan to keep Russell off the Olympic basketball team because he'd signed a professional contract, but that ended up being resolved. He was a high-level sprinter as well, so when he took off down the floor, he could easily beat other players.

There are three moments in his life that, in combination, may best define Russell: the 1969 NBA Finals, his number retirement ceremony, and the unveiling of his statue in Boston.

In 1969 Russell played his final year in the NBA. It was his least productive, and it was becoming clear that Boston's time as the league's unbeatable juggernaut was coming to an end. The Los Angeles Lakers had home court advantage, which they used to take leads of 2–0 and 3–2. Home court was being held throughout the series, which led to a lot of Lakers confidence when they went home for a deciding Game 7.

Then-owner Jack Kent Cooke was ready to make a show of what he felt like would be an inevitable Lakers victory. He put out flyers around the Forum which read:

"When, not if, the Lakers win the title, balloons [inscribed 'World Champion Lakers'] will be released from the rafters, the USC marching band will play 'Happy Days Are Here Again' and broadcaster Chick Hearn will interview [Lakers stars] Elgin Baylor, Jerry West and Wilt Chamberlain in that order."

Russell caught wind of the plan, and noticed the net full of balloons at the top of the arena.

"Those fucking balloons are staying up there," he said.

He wasn't lying.

The Celtics held off the Lakers for a 108–106 win. Russell only scored 6 points, but he had a team best 6 assists (his passing was always an underrated aspect of his career) and 21 rebounds without coming out for a rest. You can blame that one on his coach, who was also Bill Russell.

His final three years in uniform were as player-coach. There were no assistant coaches, meaning Russell had to do all the thinking of substitutions and strategy on the fly as he was playing. On top of trying to defend, rebound, and pass, he had to keep track of who had how many fouls, who was playing poorly, who was getting tired, and when to call timeouts. The game wasn't quite as complicated back then as it is now, but that's still a heavy burden for one person to bear.

After the 1969 Finals, Russell quit the game, and he quit Boston. He went on to have a mediocre coaching career with Seattle and Sacramento. He did some TV work, too, and it was during his time at ABC that Red Auerbach and the Celtics planned to retire his number.

However, Russell wanted no part of it.

"Red knows how I feel about this," Russell said. "I'm not that type of guy."

This was like two rams butting heads on a mountaintop. Auerbach was raising his number 6 on March 12, 1972, whether Russell liked it or not. So they came to an agreement.

"The only way he was going to participate would be if it was before the game," Tommy Heinsohn, then the team's head coach said. "He respected his teammates. . . . He considered the Celtics his family, so he wasn't totally averse to them doing it. But he didn't want it to happen in front of the fans."

So, in a small, private ceremony before the game, and before fans were let in, Russell stood with some of his former teammates and watched his number go into the rafters.

It wasn't until 1999, when Russell's relationship with the city itself began to thaw, that he sat for a full, actual retirement ceremony.

It's said that time heals all wounds, but it's hard to say if it's true here. It may have healed them enough for Russell to emerge from his relative solitude to become part of the NBA landscape again.

Boston's evolution in terms of racism may have helped as well. The city still has many issues as do most cities in America, but the slow march toward equality has brought the city quite a distance from what Russell endured.

The momentum to honor Russell, one of the city's truly great sports heroes, had reached a peak. A statue honoring him was finally going to be made. Many teams have honored their legends with statues outside of arenas, and Boston was on a path to do the same . . . until Russell refused.

He didn't want some ode to his individual accomplishments. He gave his approval to the honor only after it was tied to a mentoring program created for city children. The statue was placed in Boston's City Hall Plaza, symbolically near the worst images of Boston's bussing crisis. The statue is surrounded by other statues of children, and bears the inscription "There are no other people's children in the United States. There are only next-generation Americans."

These three things are Russell in a nutshell. Fiercely competitive to a point where failure simply isn't an option; fiercely private and loyal to his teammates, for whom he'd given his body and soul on the court; fiercely fighting the injustice and inequality that envelop too many.

Russell is not only a Celtics legend and he's not only a Boston legend. He's a sports legend and a human legend. He earned his Presidential Medal of Freedom many times over.

A Celtics All-Time All-Star? Yeah, he probably cemented that by 1965. They get no better than him.

Final Verdict:
Starter: Bill Russell
Backup: Robert Parish

WILD CARDS

The Candidates
Isaiah Thomas
Nate "Tiny" Archibald
Ray Allen
K. C. Jones
Rajon Rondo
Danny Ainge
Bill Sharman
Cedric Maxwell
Dennis Johnson
Tommy Heinsohn
Dave Cowens
Reggie Lewis

This is where the debate gets really fun, and a little nerve-wracking.

All these guys I just eliminated are back in contention. This is like one of those reality "redemption" shows. Except these are all guys we like.

The NBA All-Star team has 12 spots, so this one does as well. Ten of them have been filled, which means two are available for whomever I want regardless of position.

This is a lot of pressure.

The thing we need most right now is to figure out how to whittle the list down. So let's start with years of service.

Player	Years on the Celtics
Danny Ainge	8
Ray Allen	5
Tiny Archibald	5
Dave Cowens	10
Tommy Heinsohn	9
Dennis Johnson	7
K. C. Jones	9
Reggie Lewis	6
Cedric Maxwell	8
Rajon Rondo	9
Bill Sharman	10
Isaiah Thomas	3

ISAIAH THOMAS
Sigh.

I hate this part.

I hate it because I love Isaiah Thomas. I love everything he did for the Boston Celtics. He personally accelerated Boston's rebuild. There are dozens of wins on Brad Stevens's resume that are directly attributable to him.

"The one when we played Miami on the second night of a back-to-back, game 41 on December 30, was ridiculous. To this day, I'm like . . .," he said, struggling to find the right words. "I'm telling you, I came into the arena that night and I had nothing. I was gassed. I was cooked. I remember telling our assistants 'if I feel this way, I can't imagine how our team feels.' We had played the most dense schedule we had ever played up to that point, and he goes for 50. That's when I thought he's doing things that are very unusual. But it can't just be how skilled he is or how hard he works, there's gotta be a mental toughness to that that's above and beyond."

He actually went for 52. That was the night after he went for 31 against Cleveland. He averaged 30.3 points per game in that insane December. He averaged 32 the next month and 30 the month after that. He hit nearly 40 percent of his 3-pointers in that stretch!

The best I can do here is make sure you are all aware that this season is one of the most amazing single seasons in Boston Celtics history. There are few individual performances by players that equal this one.

Unfortunately, I just can't bring myself to include Isaiah Thomas as a wild card. After everything he did and after all that's happened, three years in Boston just can't crack the final two spots on this team. Not when there are so many great players—Hall of Famers—that are also on the edge.

NATE "TINY" ARCHIBALD

I swear this isn't a height thing.

Archibald is an all-time great. His pre-Celtics days were spectacular.

He just didn't do it in Boston. What he did in Boston was play a perfect role as he transitioned into the next phase of his career.

"(The Celtics were) like an Old Western—The Good, The Bad and the Ugly," Archibald said at the Naismith Memorial Basketball Hall of Fame. "Before Larry (Bird), before Kevin (McHale) and Robert (Parish), the team was the ugly. They say, 'So what was the good and the bad?' There was no good, no bad. With them, it was great. It was great because I didn't have to do a whole lot of scoring. All I needed to do was manage the game, put the ball in the right people's hands. I wished I had 10 basketballs so I could feed everyone. It was just great."

Archibald has always expressed how he's had the good fortune to play for the Celtics. For all his individual accomplishments, one goal eluded him until he came to Boston.

"Playing in the league for 14 years and not starting my career with the Celtics or did I finish my career with the Celtics—but just winning the championship and playing with, probably, some of the greatest basketball players to ever have played this game is a great feat," he told the team's official website. "But winning the championship is the all-time best memory that I will ever have."

I'm honestly happy that Archibald got his title and was able to experience the joy of all that hard work. Few players get to have that thrill.

Still, five years as a Celtic at 12.5 points and 7.1 assists aren't enough to get him on this team. They're nice numbers, but even extrapolated out to 100 possessions, he still only averaged 14.5 points and 8.1 assists per game.

It really would have been fun to have one of the little guys represented on this team. They always have to work so much harder than most players to achieve what they do. When the Sacramento Kings All-Time All-Stars book is written and they dive back into their history, Archibald will be a prime candidate for one of their spots.

This is the Celtics book. And in this book, he just doesn't make the cut.

RAY ALLEN

There are a few of you breathing a sigh of relief here. The thought of Allen making this team makes some stomachs churn in the land of beans and chowder.

Personally, I don't feel those feelings. Allen made a free agent decision that he was free to make, and part of the reason he made it was because he thought he'd been traded to Memphis.

"I got the phone call and told that I was traded for OJ Mayo," he told *Slam* magazine. "Danny Ainge and I talked and he asked me how I felt about it—I told him I was upset, that I couldn't believe it. I said, 'I can't knock you, you have to do what you do for your team. I understand it's a business [and] there's nothing I can do about it.' He was like, 'Well, I'll be in touch.' I told my family we've been traded to Memphis. One of my sons said, 'Don't worry about it Dad, we're Grizzlies fans now. We're gonna make this work.' I took that into my summer, that I could potentially—regardless of what I did for the team, there's no great loyalty shown amongst the teams to the players, 'cause they'll trade you in a heartbeat. When they trade you, they'll tell you, 'We're a team but we have to do what's best for our squad.' As a player if we want more money or ask for a trade we are looked upon as being greedy, or disloyal."

Neither side is wrong, here. Fans have every right to be upset when a player leaves, though some amount of understanding would be good, too. Players have every right to choose where they work. Free agency is something they've earned, and if a player isn't happy somewhere for whatever reason, he can change his situation when his contract is up. Teams also have the right to trade players as they see fit.

This is part of the deal everyone signs up for in the NBA. You can be hired, fired, and traded on a whim. You can be happy one season and pissed off the next. Circumstances change.

They changed for Allen in Boston and he moved on at a time when another year or two in Boston might have cemented a long-term legacy. Unlike Archibald, his per 100 possession numbers are spectacular.

Allen averaged 16.7 points per game and shot nearly 41 percent from deep, an absurdly good number. He averaged 24.8 points per 100 possessions, though, which just goes to show how much of a sacrifice he made coming to Boston.

"Everyone's got to sacrifice. If you think about it, all of their shots were cut from the year before," Doc Rivers said before a game in Boston as Clippers coach. "Every single player on the team, not just Ray, Paul (Pierce) and Kevin (Garnett), but Rondo's shots were down, Perk (Kendrick Perkins)—well, he thought he should shoot more—but his shots were down. Everyone's shots. You can't just get something when you're trying to win something. And then the sacrifice is what bonds you together a lot, and so our guys all sacrificed, but Ray clearly sacrificed the most."

The year before joining Boston, a 31-year-old Allen averaged 26.4 points per game, while adding 4.5 rebounds, 4.1 assists, and 1.5 steals. He was a Western Conference All-Star who took 21 shots per game.

He took 13.5 shots per game in Boston his first year, and 12.5 overall in his five years here. Allen slowly morphed from primary scorer to almost exclusively a 3-point shooting threat as he aged. The reason why he was still elite at that as a Celtic was because of his meticulous workout regimen and preparation.

No one prepared like Allen. No one. His pregame routine was more precise than anything a Swiss watchmaker can create. Each step, each shot, each drill was executed to his own perfectionist standards. He built a muscle memory that allowed him to hit ridiculous shots.

His signature moment with the Celtics may have been the Game 4 clinching layup in the 2008 NBA Finals against the Los Angeles Lakers. Boston had overcome the biggest deficit in NBA Finals history and they were up three with 20 seconds left. With four seconds on the shot clock, Allen looked Sasha Vujacic square in the eyes, hit him with a hesitation, blew by him on the right, then crossed over to finish on the left side to avoid a late challenge by Pau Gasol.

He made it a five-point game with 16.4 seconds left. They ended up winning by six, and it was a crucial victory that gave the Celtics a 3–1 series lead. Had they lost, the series would have been tied at two games apiece with Game 5 in Los Angeles.

Boston lost Game 5, and it's hard to say if they would have had they lost Game 4. If they did, the Lakers could have gone back to Boston with a 3–2 lead rather than a 3–2 deficit.

Allen got his first ring in Boston that season. He deserves consideration here as a key contributor to a champion, but, frankly, there are a lot of key contributors to champions being left off this team. That's part of it when it comes to a debate like this with the Celtics.

Like Archibald, Allen could very well make another team's All-Time All-Star list. His seven seasons in Milwaukee were extraordinary. His five in Seattle were brilliant. His five in Boston were very good, but not quite as good as those, and thus not quite good enough to make this team.

So we've whittled three away. I've got thoughts on what to do next but those can be deceiving. I need to look at some numbers. So let's try looking at the remaining nine candidates with some basic, leveled-out numbers.

Note: I'm using "true shooting percentage" rather than field goal percentage as a bit of leveler. True shooting percentage is a metric that factors in free throw shooting and 3-point shooting as well as standard field goal percentage. I think it's important to use this across generations because while some of the earlier players shot poorly from the field, that was largely a function of how the game was played. Some of the big scorers of the early days had great free throw percentages but no 3-point line, but this number sort of evens things out.

Player	Points per game	Rebounds per game	Assists per game	True shooting percentage
Danny Ainge	14.4	3.5	5.6	.555
Dave Cowens	16.6	12.8	3.6	.496
Tommy Heinsohn	22.8	10.7	2.5	.460
K. C. Jones	10.3	4.9	6.0	.435
Dennis Johnson	13.4	3.5	6.8	.510
Reggie Lewis	19.4	4.8	2.8	.538
Cedric Maxwell	16.2	7.8	2.7	.637
Rajon Rondo	12.0	5.2	9.3	.507
Bill Sharman	20.3	4.4	3.4	.497

It seems as if we've got ourselves a couple more eliminations.

K. C. JONES

If this book was called the All-Time Defensive All-Stars, then Jones would have a spot. He's as accomplished as anyone comes, with two NCAA titles, an Olympic Gold Medal, eight championships as a player, two as an assistant coach, and two as a head coach. He's a Hall of Famer.

I spent a lot of time writing about the racism Bill Russell faced and overcame throughout his playing days. Jones was right there with him. They were teammates in San Francisco and Boston, and Jones wasn't immune to the hatred.

"We were living in Framingham when I was a player," Jones told *Boston* magazine. "I went to buy a house about five blocks away.... The neighbors said they didn't want any blacks to move into the house."

Jones made it clear that he harbors no hatred toward the city and he generally enjoyed his time in Boston, but that doesn't mean it didn't make life tough on him as well.

K. C. Jones's overall contributions to the Celtics deserve some sort of special recognition. He was part of 12 championship teams in some capacity.

I guess this section, as well as his coaching section, will have to suffice. It's important to mention his role in Celtics history, but that's about as far as it goes as far as this book is concerned. He's not going to make it as a player.

RAJON RONDO

Rondo's best days were his Celtics days. He finished his time in Boston with four All-Star appearances, one championship, one All-Rookie, four All-Defense, and one All-NBA nod all within nine seasons.

Two things derailed his career: his ACL injury and his stubbornness. Rondo's injury came during his fourth-straight All-Star season. He was averaging 11.1 assists at the time, but the Celtics were in the throes of their last gasps of the new Big 3 era.

Allen had already left and the Celtics were relying on a hodgepodge of bench players to try to re-create the specialist roles around Garnett and Pierce.

They were streaky, too. Rondo's injury came at the end of a six-game losing streak, which followed a six-game winning streak and preceded a seven-game winning streak. They had bursts, but Rondo's clashing with players and his coach had made everything more tedious than it should have been.

"He's a very competitive player. He can rub you the wrong way if you're not careful," said his former teammate and 2008 champion, Leon Powe. "If you're thinking he's just talking to you all types of different ways—no. He's really talking to you to get on you, but he wants you to do better so the team can do better. But he's got different ways of saying it. He'll get on you in the harshest way possible. He don't sugar coat it."

Powe's quote in the point guard section of this book where he says Rondo knows everything is the best summation of the flashy Kentucky product. He pissed off Tubby Smith in college and he pissed off Doc Rivers in the pros, and it's because Rondo just sees the floor differently.

I'm a firm believer in the concept of your biggest strength being your biggest weakness. Rondo's basketball IQ is off the charts. He sees things in four dimensions while we see them in three. What he wasn't able to do was figure out how to make that work for everyone in the room with him. He got frustrated and decided to do things his way.

There was a short time where his way worked. There was a time when Rondo was on a path that, if you squinted, you could see led to challenging Bob Cousy's greatness somewhere down the line. In that universe, I'd be debating Jo Jo White in this section.

That's a shame because (a) there's nothing worse to me in basketball than unrealized potential, and (b) it would have made my life a whole lot easier in this section. Jo Jo is awesome and he'd be on this team no matter what.

Rondo could have been one of the All-Time All-Stars. He could have been a starter. Instead, he's being eliminated.

I do love that his middle name is Pierre, though. That's fun.

DANNY AINGE

I have to be nice to him here because he still runs the team and I still need quotes from him.

My favorite photo of Ainge is him standing with a ball tucked under his arm, a hand on his hip, and wearing a shirt that says "I hate Danny Ainge." He reveled in the hatred he caused by playing the game.

"I'm just the type of player you like to have on your team, but that you don't like to play against. That's perfectly OK with me," he once told the *Los Angeles Times*. "I don't want the players I play against to like me. I mean, I want them to like me, but I don't want them to like playing against me.

"I want them to think I'm going to bug them all night. That's my objective. Bill Walton told me when he first got here, 'If you're not getting booed on the road, then you're not doing your job.'"

Ainge, like nearly everyone in this book it seems, almost took a very different path. He was drafted by the Toronto Blue Jays to play second base, but that didn't quite work out. Boston wanted him so badly that Red Auerbach took the Blue Jays to court and the Celtics paid half a million dollars to buy out his contract to get him to play basketball.

Once in Boston he was a great complement to the Big 3. Not only was his shooting needed to space the floor, his dogged determination and irritating effort helped give the Celtics an edge. His reputation took a hit when Don Nelson, a former Celtic himself, called Ainge a "cheap shot artist." Ainge's coach at the time, K. C. Jones, took great exception to that.

"I can understand trying to get an edge in a series, to try and get an advantage, which is what he (Nelson) was doing," Jones told the *Los Angeles Times*, "but you can't do it at the expense of somebody's reputation. You don't ever hear that about players like (Detroit center Bill) Laimbeer.

"When I was playing, I was very stoic," Jones said. "I was mean and determined and sneaky. I pestered people, and they didn't like that. Danny has that same troubled-brow look. He's all over the place. He's a lot of me.

"In my opinion, all he's done is just play hard."

He played hard his entire time in Boston. He made an All-Star team and won two rings with the Celtics. He accepted the 3-point line before most of his contemporaries, launching more than four per game by his final year in Boston.

He was traded to Sacramento in 1989. He had a few good years with the Celtics as a player, and he's enjoying a good run as the team's president of basketball operations. His reputation as "trader Danny" and embracing of the cold business side fits his "do what you gotta do to win" mentality. Trades are nothing personal, it's just business.

So is this.

Danny, you're off the team.

Let's reassess who we have left.

Three of Dave Cowens, Tommy Heinsohn, Dennis Johnson, Reggie Lewis, Cedric Maxwell, and Bill Sharman have to go. At this point, it's hard to make statistical arguments. We're crossing too many generations and a lot of data that could be helpful isn't available from those old box scores.

We're getting down to the art of this: the nuance of trying to make sense of eras and challenges.

OK, here we go with more cuts.

BILL SHARMAN

This is a tough one because the numbers point to utter domination. He's an eight-time All-Star who averaged 18 points a game and won four championships. I'm a moron for not putting him in this, right?

I just can't bring myself to do it. He's a 6'1" shooting guard who flourished in the earliest days of the NBA and, while he certainly is worthy of consideration here, I just don't think he is better than the remaining players.

I want to be clear here. I believe the best players of any generation would be able to play in any other generation if given the same advantages of that time period. Sharman could have gone to the 1980s and, given the money and focus on the sport, figured out how to play and play well.

The question I have to answer here is whether he's better than Dave Cowens, Tommy Heinsohn, Dennis Johnson, Reggie Lewis, and Cedric Maxwell.

Well, Cowens and Heinsohn also scored, and he rebounded as well. Johnson didn't score as much as a Celtic, but he could have if the situation were different and his overall shooting was better. Lewis did bits of everything, and Maxwell basically didn't miss.

Sharman is one of the pillars of the early Celtics, and guess what? He also could have taken a different path.

He spent five years in the Brooklyn Dodgers farm system. He got a call-up early in his career and was caught up in a brawl that day, thus creating the legend that Sharman is the only man to have been ejected from a major-league game without ever playing in a major-league game.

Sharman was actually a two-sport athlete, playing for the Celtics at the same time. His baseball career went nowhere and he dedicated himself to basketball in 1955.

The basebrawl wasn't his only dalliance in the art of in-game brouhahas.

"Bill was tough," Lakers legend Jerry West told the *Los Angeles Times*. "I'll tell you this, you did not drive by him. He got into more fights than Mike Tyson. You respected him as a player."

This is a difficult decision, but, then again, it's not supposed to be easy to pick this team. The Boston Celtics are a legendary franchise and I've still got three more players to eliminate.

Sharman was tough, he scored a ton, and he won championships, but I'm leaving him off the All-Time All-Star team.

CEDRIC MAXWELL

Mr. "climb on my back, boys" isn't going to be on this team. He's a Finals MVP, and in 1984 he turned in a classic Game 7 performance in a 111–102 win over the Los Angeles Lakers for Boston's 15th championship. He took 17 free throws in that game, giving the Lakers fits as they tried to guard him.

(Side note: He refutes ever saying "climb on my back, boys." He does admit he said something similar, but it was much more vulgar than that cleaned up version.)

"The thing about the seventh game, there is no wiggle room. Everything multiplies tenfold," he once told the *Boston Globe*. "Everything's magnified because of what's at stake. It's going to be a defining legacy for these guys."

Max was never shy about anything. He never feared any moment in a game, nor did he fear any opponent, especially one in purple and gold.

"There was a time, if I saw a Laker on fire and I was holding a glass of water, I'd drink the water," he told the *Los Angeles Times*. "There was a time where I couldn't say Kareem Abdul-Jabbar without throwing up."

Maxwell was an old-school forward who was deadly from within 12 feet, and who is still one of the most accurate scorers in team history. He was an underrated passer and defender and he often checked the opponent's best wing.

He was an underrated player in general. He's one of the best forwards the Celtics have ever had. If I was putting together a trash-talk team, he would be in the starting five. He still, to this day, patrols the TD Garden before games talking smack here and there. Maxwell, now on the Celtics radio broadcast, will spend time going back and forth with former players who are now on other team broadcasts. Hell, he's even talking smack in the media dining room.

Max is an all-time character, and he's had some amazing seasons for the Celtics. It's wonderful that his rift with the team was patched so he could do the broadcasts and be appreciated by a new generation of fans.

Unfortunately, he's not an All-Time All-Star.

The remaining players are Dave Cowens, Tommy Heinsohn, Dennis Johnson, and Reggie Lewis. This is where things really get hard. I've got an MVP, an eight-time champion, the glue that held the Big 3 era together, and a phenom lost in his prime.

The bottom line here is that All-Stars put up numbers. Three of these guys simply put up better numbers than the other, which brings me to my most painful cut of them all.

DENNIS JOHNSON

When I first visualized this project, I thought DJ was getting in for sure. But I'm a child of the '80s Celtics. I cut my teeth learning the game from Johnson's C's.

There was no way I could leave a key member of those amazing Celtics teams off, right?

The deeper we dive into Celtics past, the more amazing players we find. The '70s-era Celtics are particularly short-changed because '70s-era basketball is sort of the lost decade. The league truly was in danger back then, and it was lucky to survive, but the waning fan interest meant less of a focus on some of the best to ever play the game. Once that reminder is made, a guy like Johnson gets pushed off a list like this.

If you're expecting this to be the spot where I say the guy almost didn't make it as a Celtic . . . you're right.

He hardly played in high school and he was working a blue-collar job when the coach at Los Angeles Harbor College saw him playing defense in a pickup game and asked him to enroll. After a couple of years he got national attention and found his way to Pepperdine, but that never would have happened had Jim White not been at that court, at that time, to catch Johnson in that game.

If White had gotten a phone call, hit a red light, or eaten a bad burrito, his day would have been disrupted and Johnson might never have existed in the basketball lexicon.

Maybe it was that late start that caused him to mature more slowly in the NBA. He never really had to learn how to be a teammate or how to be coached. He was a problem at every stop until he got to Boston.

"When I found out I got traded from Phoenix, Red Auerbach told me, 'You're the final piece to the puzzle,' which is a nice thing to hear," Johnson told *Slam* magazine's Alan Paul. "On the second day of training camp, we separated into teams and I was with Larry (Bird), Robert (Parish) and Cedric (Maxwell), and it just clicked immediately. Everyone there knew that we were going to have something pretty special. We had such intense battles through camp, you were kind of glad to play the first regular-season game. We just blitzed people, and everyone knew that they better bring their A-game against us and it still might not be enough."

The thing he needed to do, and the thing that's keeping him off this team, is sacrifice.

"I never had a problem. There were enough shots to go around," he said in that same interview. "I averaged about 15 a game, down from 19 or 20 in Phoenix, and that was fine. It was so much fun. My role was to set it up, make the right passes to Larry, Kevin, Robert and Cedric, get eight or nine assists, hit the shots when they were there and play great defense."

This is why I both have to cut Johnson from consideration and hate doing it. He is the exact kind of player every loaded team needs. He was a great individual player who took a step back because he recognized how much better everyone else was. I'm not building a basketball team, though. I'm putting together an All-Star team. I'm not considering fit and skills and who will execute a game plan better. That would be a much different debate, and I can guarantee you I'd have DJ on that one.

He's not on this one. And I'm going to stop writing about it or else I'm going to make myself cry.

We're almost there, so I'm going to pull another classic reality show move and instead of cutting one more guy, I'm going to tell you which one of these three guys is making it, then I'll decide which of the last two is in.

This is what's called building suspense (or being an asshole—I've been accused of both).

In: Tommy Heinsohn

Red Auerbach once said Heinsohn had the oldest 27-year-old body he's ever seen. The boisterous Heinsohn was happy to have his fun, smoke a cigarette, and have a beer. He was also the target of Red's ire on more than one occasion.

Red knew he could do that to Heinsohn without it bothering him. He couldn't ride Bob Cousy that way. Heinsohn, though, was a tough SOB. Though he did get tired of it from time to time.

"I went up to him and I said, 'hey Red, let me ask you a question, do I deserve to be on this team?' and he says 'why you sure do, Tommy,'" he once recalled. "I said 'do I deserve to be a starter on this team?' and he says 'absolutely.' I said, 'well Red, if that'd be the case, I need you to get off my back a little bit and start pointing it in other directions, because the rookies on this team are starting to steal my socks.'"

Stolen hosiery aside, Heinsohn is often one of the team's more underrated star players. Fans see him as a fun, sometimes bombastic sportscaster and they don't really fully grasp his greatness. Heinsohn played on great teams with great players, but he held his own.

"I was the bail out offensive player," Heinsohn once said. "When a play would break down, the Celtics all knew I could get a shot off."

Often that shot was a hook, and he mastered how to score with it well before Lew Alcindor came into the league. He was a skilled offensive player, even though he might have thought he was even more skilled than he was.

The occasional bad shot was tolerated because not only would Heinsohn score enough points to make up for it, he was tough and unafraid to mix it up.

"Tommy Heinsohn played with the gruffness of a dock worker," Bill Russell once said of his teammate.

Heinsohn would take advantage of space created by Russell and muscle his way to the rim for offensive rebounds. He'd knock guys around defensively. He was emotional, and that worked to his advantage.

In one of his many stories, he was tasked with setting a pick on Wilt Chamberlain after a free throw so Bill Russell could streak downcourt. He'd have to get into Wilt's way on every free throw, which is basically the basketball version of asking a guy to obscure the path of a moose in heat.

"Finally, he gets wise to what I'm doing. And he says, 'You do that one more time and I'm going to knock you on your ass,'" Heinsohn said. "So, you know, you never back down. I looked him in the eye and I said, 'Bring your lunch.'"

Allow me this Ferris Bueller–like fourth-wall break as I squint and cock my head at "bring your lunch." I guess trash-talk was different in the '60s.

So Heinsohn sets a pick on Chamberlain and Wilt brought his lunch. Wilt also broke his hand in the ensuing fracas, courtesy of Tom Gola's especially hard skull. Tommy the instigator got the job done.

His numbers speak for themselves. On a team with Cousy, Sharman, and Sam Jones, Heinsohn still managed to find a way to put the ball in the basket. He could raise his game in the playoffs, averaging nearly 19 points and 9 rebounds and winning championships in all but one season.

He fit perfectly with the group, giving it not only the scoring, rebounding, and toughness that they needed, but also a fair amount of levity.

Tommy Heinsohn has, somehow, been a part of every one of Boston's 17 championships. He's also going to be part of the All-Time All-Star team.

And so now it comes down to two. Dave Cowens vs. Reggie Lewis. One spot left on the team. Let's take one last look at them both.

DAVE COWENS

The fourth pick in 1970 knew what he was getting into with Heinsohn and the Celtics.

"I'd played up-tempo in high school and college, and my conditioning was at a very high level," he told author Michael D. McClellan. "I was used to pushing through various thresholds of pain and fatigue, even when other players were having trouble. The league at that time suited my style perfectly."

That high-motor led him to places only the greatest greats went. In 1973 he was both the All-Star and the league MVP, something only Cousy and Russell had done until that point.

The high-motor also led to a lot of fouls. In fact, he led the team in fouls for three years.

It's tough to say a 6'9" dude had a Napoleon complex, but for NBA centers, he wasn't particularly big. His opponents were, though, and Cowens's chest puffed out when it came time to face them.

"It was always a challenge to stop them," he said. "Bob Lanier, Wilt Chamberlain, Kareem, Bob Bellamy, Willis Reed—every night it was a completely different style, a different matchup, but all of these guys could score. That was the one constant."

Cowens banged with the biggest of them all at the time, and wore them down. They say a perpetual motion machine can't be built, but I'd submit one already has in Cowens.

"The look in his eyes is something that I can't find words to adequately describe," his former teammate Paul Westphal once said. "You had to see that look for yourself to know what I'm talking about. It was scary. He was so focused on the game."

REGGIE LEWIS

Lewis presents the hardest of challenges here.

We lost him in his prime, and as such there are no guarantees about what his future might have been. We don't know if there would have been a fall, or an on-court injury, or anything that hampered his performance. All we know is who he was when he died.

"I remember talking to people [about] Reggie; there's no better first step in basketball," his college coach Jim Calhoun, who then coached Northeastern, told the *Boston Globe*. "That quiet confidence, I never knew where it came from, I really didn't. But he had it and it was rare and once he got his opportunity. He was a unique, unique kid."

He had to earn his place on the Celtics. His rookie year began months after Boston had lost the 1987 championship to Magic Johnson and the Los Angeles Lakers. Few people saw him as any kind of franchise savior at the time. He was the 22nd overall pick: a skinny kid out of Northeastern, a short drive from the Boston Garden.

His college career was stellar, but no one came out of Northeastern. At that point he was the fourth Huskies player to make the NBA and none of the other three lasted more than two seasons.

He was, obviously, the best of them, though. And it didn't take long for him to make an impact. After barely playing in his rookie year, Lewis broke into the rotation and immediately paid dividends.

"It's great to have the respect of all your teammates, especially the Big 3," he once said. "If it wasn't for them, I wouldn't be here today. Before I can become the leader of the team, I have to get their respect. That's something that I worked hard for and now that I have it, I have to make sure that I continue to improve my game."

He improved it to a point where he was averaging nearly 21 points a game in the two seasons prior to his death.

"I think it's obvious to anyone who would look that this was a loss that created holes in our game, if you will, at every level," former Celtics general manager Jan Volk said. "Combined with the loss of Len Bias, that right there, the two of them would have been a dynamic duo, there's no doubt about it."

Bias was a phenom drafted second overall by the Celtics the year before Lewis was drafted. He died of a cocaine overdose. The long Celtics malaise of the '90s and early 2000s was a direct result of these two deaths.

So where does that leave us for this last spot?

I walked into this debate convinced I was going to give it to Lewis. I was sure that the talent he had was going to win out. In my mind, before looking back over things one last time, I felt like Lewis and what he represented needed to be part of this team.

There is no doubt in my mind that he was on a Hall of Fame track. There's no doubt in my mind that his number would have been raised into the rafters no matter what.

I sat down here to write about Lewis earning this spot, but I just can't do it.

Cowens's best five-year stretch is just better than Lewis's. Hell, Cowens's worst five-year stretch isn't that far off from Lewis. Cowens was an MVP, a Rookie of the Year, and a two-time champion. He made three All-NBA teams and eight All-Star teams.

I can sit here and tell you in my heart of hearts that Reggie Lewis would have been a better player than Cowens had he lived. I can believe it with every fiber of my being, and I do.

But he never got the chance. The legend of Reggie Lewis is an important one to remember, but the career of Dave Cowens is just too good to pass on for what we're recognizing here.

Final Verdict:
Tommy Heinsohn
Dave Cowens

COACH

The Candidates
Brad Stevens
Doc Rivers
K. C. Jones
Tommy Heinsohn
Red Auerbach

The head coach's job has changed a lot over the years. There was once a time when they didn't have assistants. The coach ran the whole show, which is almost impossible to do nowadays. The last two coaches to try running a team and coaching it, Doc Rivers with the Los Angeles Clippers and Stan Van Gundy with the Detroit Pistons, were overwhelmed by the job.

The league has become very complicated over the years. The amount of money involved has changed the dynamics to a point where what the coach does and how he does it are significantly different.

You might think it's much simpler than that. In the levels below the NBA, and in the older days of the league, it was. The coach's word was final, and anyone who didn't like it could pound sand.

Now it's a players' league. A general manager could give a coach a team that just doesn't fit well, and when it doesn't work well, it's the coach that gets canned. Players make so much money that the investment in them trumps the investment in the coaches. And with free agency, something that didn't exist in Auerbach's day, players can exert some pressure on teams to bring in coaches that they like.

The style of play has also evolved immensely over the years. The 3-point line and its impact on the calculus of winning basketball has changed coaching strategies. The days of dominant big men have fallen by the wayside and a guard-driven offense has risen from its ashes. Where once the term "scoring point guard" was almost pejorative, a point guard who doesn't score nowadays is seen as more of a liability. Steph Curry and James Harden would have been a shooting guard and small forward in older times, but both are point guards in today's NBA.

That means coaching has to be more creative not only in how to utilize those kinds of players, but also in how to stop them. Where once there were no assistants, there now can be six or more. Each has a specific role in things like player development and offensive and defensive assignments.

All this is well and good. Yeah, things have changed over the years, but one thing has not: The coach's goal is always finding ways to win. Whether it's alone or with a bunch of assistants, with free agents or not, the coach's job is to find a way to raise banners.

Boston has 17 of them up there, and they've gotten close to a lot more.

BRAD STEVENS

Three hundred wins is the cutoff for consideration, and Stevens just made the cut in the 2019-20 season.

It's not easy to make the jump from college to the NBA, but Stevens has done it very successfully. His first two seasons were the only two losing seasons of his career. Until the 2018-19 season, he'd increased his win total each year from the previous year.

You can count Stevens among those in Celtics history who almost didn't make it in basketball at all. He was a standout in high school and he had a good Division III career, but he took a job at Eli Lilly after graduation. He did well there, and he was making good money for a kid out of college. They liked him and he probably could have had a very nice life in Indiana with his wife and family had he stayed.

He just loved basketball too much. He had people in his orbit still in basketball and, ultimately, he landed an unpaid assistant job at Butler University. That quickly became a paid spot and, with some help from assistant Todd Lickliter, Stevens figured out how he needed to approach the game to be successful.

Stevens was meticulous, and his focus was on the smallest details. He developed his lust for the process of winning basketball. When Lickliter became head coach at Butler, he gave Stevens, his protégé, a full-time job as an assistant.

"Nobody has had a bigger influence on me as far as day-to-day preparation than Todd Lickliter," Stevens once told the *Boston Globe*. "He was a huge, huge, huge influence."

Eventually Lickliter left Butler for Iowa, and Stevens got the head coaching job at Butler. He won 30 games twice and amassed a 166-49 record. He took Butler to two national championship games, one of which was nearly won on a Gordon Hayward halfcourt heave.

He joined the Boston Celtics in 2013 and quickly developed a reputation for overachieving. After a wild first season that saw 19 players come through Boston through four huge trades (including the Kevin Garnett/Paul Pierce trade a week after he was hired), Stevens and the Celtics haven't missed the playoffs.

Part of Stevens's brilliance is his knack for out of timeout plays, which are great not because of some grand innovation, but because they take advantage of a little wrinkle he noticed in real time. Some of them are actually very simple, but their precision makes them perfect.

"Some of the plays he draws up, we kind of look at them like, 'I don't really know if this is going to work or not,'" Marcus Smart once told SB Nation's Paul Flannery. "And when you do it, you're like, 'You know what, sorry I ever doubted you.' When you have a coach like that, it's fun to play for, and you want to go out there and give it everything you have."

This was on display in the 2018 playoffs against the Philadelphia 76ers. With Boston down one with eight seconds left in overtime, Stevens drew up a play that actually got four Sixers defenders to chase their assignments and leave the Celtics basket. Not only that, but he got Philly to switch Joel Embiid off Al Horford so he was fronted by a smaller defender. With no one between him and the basket, the pass was lofted over his shoulder so he could catch it NFL receiver–style and he laid the ball in for the win.

The play didn't require elaborate screening or crazy actions. Stevens simply knew the Sixers were switching everything, so he could dictate the defensive matchup. He knew they were aggressively denying, so running players toward the ball but also out to halfcourt would clear space for Horford.

Brilliant simplicity.

If there's a knock on Stevens it's that he has not yet, as of the 2020 season anyway, been able to figure out how to manage a big-ego superstar. If there's a recipe for great coaching in the NBA, Stevens is still missing a dash of Phil Jackson.

Don't get me wrong, every player in the NBA comes in with some level of ego. It's hard to function in the NBA at any level without some of that. But the biggest egos require some delicate handling. Jackson's strength was figuring out how to get the biggest of them to mesh long enough to bear championship fruit.

Stevens had two years of Kyrie Irving, and those only bore unrealized expectations. Undoubtedly, Stevens is using those two seasons as data points for the next time. After losing to the Milwaukee Bucks in the 2019 playoffs, a forlorn Stevens admitted to his own failures.

"I've been a coach for 12 years and we let go of the rope and cracked more than we probably should have. And we need to be better than that," he said. "I'll be the first to say that as far as any other year that I've been a head coach it's certainly been the most trying. I think I did a bad job. Like, at the end of the day, as a coach, if your team doesn't find its best fit together that's on you. So I'll do a lot of deep dives into how I can be better."

He started the next season saying, "I just think all that I've always thought and believed about the game has just been reinforced." Time will tell if that lesson will turn into championships. Fair or not, that's how success is measured for coaches in Boston. Stevens certainly seems to have what it takes to get there.

Ten years from now if this book is rewritten, maybe Stevens makes this more of a debate. For now, Stevens will be a talented onlooker.

Doc Rivers

Rivers joined the Celtics with a Coach of the Year award already under his belt, so he arrived with expectations. He also showed up at the most anxious time in Celtics history.

It is understandably arrogant to say Celtics fans were upset with an 18-year championship drought. There are teams without a single title at all, or who still have been waiting decades for one. The last time the Hawks won a title, their team was in St. Louis, so I get any eye-rolling from non-Celtics fans.

Still, that's what Rivers walked into. The team had moved far enough away from the Rick Pitino debacle to refocus on the task at hand, but Rivers was asked to win more than a title. He had to win over the team's best player.

Paul Pierce was at the height of his petulance when Rivers arrived. His reputation was already damaged by Team USA's performance in the 2002 World Championships, where they casually, cockily, waltzed to a sixth-place finish. Pierce did little in the ensuing years to repair that, and he reached his nadir after he was ejected during a playoff series against Indiana.

Eventually, as noted in the Small Forward chapter, he and Rivers had a come-to-Jesus moment, which led to Rivers's first victory in Boston.

Rivers won Coach of the Year in Orlando by taking a team that was picked to finish last to a .500 record. He didn't win the award with the Celtics, despite winning 66 games in his first year and taking Boston to a championship. (SHAKA VIA WIKIMEDIA COMMONS)

With a recommitted superstar, Danny Ainge and the Celtics decided to retool around him rather than move him and start over. They acquired Ray Allen and Kevin Garnett.

Now Rivers had his next challenge. How was he going to mold this collection of number one options into a cohesive team?

An already scheduled preseason tour of Europe helped. The team bonded in the confines of their Rome hotel, aided by Rivers preaching of the team concept.

When they broke huddles, they said "1, 2, 3, Ubuntu." Rivers introduced the team to ubuntu, an African philosophical concept of being through others: "I am, because we are."

Garnett, the most unselfish of superstars, latched onto it. To say he embraced it would be wrong. It enveloped him like the Marvel Comics character Venom. Rivers rode Garnett's passion to full control of his veteran-laden team. He stepped back when needed, allowing the trio of future Hall of Famers to police themselves. He stepped into guide them when something was going astray. Rivers, a former player himself, understood what they needed and gave it to them.

"Playing for Doc was fun. He leads you. He's a leader," said former Celtic Leon Powe. "He makes you want to run through a brick wall for him. No matter the circumstance, no matter how tall the task may be, you want to play for that guy, because he instills confidence in you as well. He knows how to motivate you."

Rivers stands in contrast to Stevens. Rivers isn't quite as meticulous, but that's what made him right for this team. They didn't need a coach to put them here or there. They needed a coach that kept the atom from splitting. He created a containment system that took volatile ingredients and focused them into a powerful weapon, which earned him his second victory.

The 2008 Celtics beat the Los Angeles Lakers for a championship. It was a full-circle moment for Rivers and Pierce. The image of Pierce dousing Rivers with a Gatorade bath is burned in the memories of Celtics fans lucky enough to witness it.

Rivers is a motivator who coaches more by feel than metrics. He figures out where people's buttons are and he pushes them. One of the best stories of Rivers's motivation came when he took $100 from everyone—coaches, players, and staff included—and hid it in a ceiling at the Staples Center in Los Angeles in February of 2010.

"I actually thought we were losing hope," Rivers told *Sports Illustrated* in 2015. "So this was one of those things that wasn't pre-planned, it was instinctive. . . . It was just a gut move. I thought the Lakers would be in the NBA Finals, and the only way to play them again was to get there with them."

Twenty-six hundred dollars sat in that ceiling for months without being noticed. Boston did, in fact, make it back to the Staples Center that June. Unfortunately for Rivers, injuries cost Boston for the second-straight year, and they lost that series to Kobe Bryant and the Lakers.

Things never quite got back on track for the Celtics, and it didn't take long for the volatility to become too much. Ray Allen and Rajon Rondo privately feuded. Kendrick Perkins was traded away. His replacement, an aging Shaquille O'Neal, was never able to contribute as much as they needed him to.

Allen soon left for the Miami Heat, a betrayal in the eyes of his former Ubuntu brothers. Those Heat, now with LeBron James, Chris Bosh, and Dwyane Wade, overtook Boston as the Eastern Conference power.

The end was obvious at this point. The only question was how this era would die. Would Rivers get to ride with Pierce into the sunset, or would the cold business of NBA basketball take hold?

Rivers knew the answer. So did Pierce.

Rivers forced his way out of Boston, which caused many Celtics fans to turn on him. He, too, was a traitor just like Allen was. He betrayed the family and was written off by those who felt spurned.

It was Rivers's departure that opened the door for Stevens. Pierce and Garnett were traded for pieces that ultimately became a core to a resurgent Celtics team under Stevens. Things worked out.

Provincialism in sports prevents many from getting over it though, which is a shame. Rivers was as much a part of that 2008 victory as any player. Maybe if they'd had better injury luck, Rivers would have three rings instead of one.

He doesn't, but that one was a good one. Unfortunately for Rivers, it's not quite good enough to crack the top two in Boston Celtics history.

Grab a seat next to Stevens, Doc. And save some room.

K. C. Jones

Jones was a tough SOB as a player, and he could be the same as a coach, but only selectively. For Jones, who always seemed measured on the sidelines, an outburst meant something was exceptionally wrong.

"K. C. never coached out of fear, the way some coaches do," Red Auerbach said after Jones's retirement from coaching. "He coached out of confidence. Everybody thinks K. C. is this calm, cool, low-key guy. The truth is, it hurts him as much as anybody to lose."

Auerbach appreciated Jones's demeanor because the general lack of ranting and raving made the few times he lost his cool more effective. When it came time to get a strong point across, the meltdown got attention. For stronger personalities, Red thought, constant ranting and raving lost its effectiveness quickly.

Jones is one of many former Celtics players to become a coach. Auerbach had an affinity for his own guys, choosing to trust those with whom he'd built a relationship to run the teams he built as an executive.

He began his coaching career in the ABA five years after retiring from the Celtics. He quickly moved to the NBA, where he led the 1975 Washington Bullets past the Celtics to the NBA Finals, where they were swept by the Golden State Warriors.

He was fired after the next season, and joined the Celtics as an assistant coach, first under former teammate Tommy Heinsohn and then under Satch Sanders. Bill Fitch took the team over in the 1979-80 season, Larry Bird's rookie year. The team won a title in 1981 and Jones took the team over in 1983 after Fitch resigned over Harry Mangurian's sale of the team.

"K. C. Jones was the nicest man I ever met in my life," Larry Bird once said. "I was fortunate to have him coach me for five or six years." Bird also once joked, "He's the kind of person I'd like to be, but I don't have the time to work at it."

Jones was fortunate to walk into a ready-made winner. The Celtics Big 3 was well-established and Bird was at the height of his powers, winning the first of his three-straight league MVPs. Jones won a championship in his first year at the helm, and in 1986, he would beat his former boss Fitch for another.

Much like Rivers, Jones understood what it took for superstars to function on the court. He played under Auerbach, and with Bob Cousy, Bill Russell, Sam Jones, and Tommy Heinsohn. He was a hard-nosed role player, and he quickly learned what made his star teammates tick. In some ways, he was Rivers before Rivers, down to the buy-in from the team's best player. Bird publicly said Jones had his and the team's respect, and that was all that was ever needed.

"I listen to the players," Jones said. "My job is to give them direction and a base to operate from, but you have to let them use their own creativity and imaginations. It's their game, they have to be allowed to play it."

The knock on Jones is that he rode Bird, Parish, and McHale to most of his coaching success. That might or might not be true, but it can also be said of every good coach. Where would Auerbach have been without Russell and Cousy? Where would Phil Jackson have been without Michael Jordan and Scottie Pippen, or Kobe Bryant and Shaquille O'Neal?

"It was the best," he said of inheriting that team. "It was my first year as head coach and we weren't supposed to win. It was big in all aspects, big in every sense of the word."

Jones won 308 regular-season games in five seasons as Celtics coach. He's got two titles. Maybe Gary Payton, who publicly flogged Jones for his coaching in two seasons in Seattle, will disagree, but the results speak for themselves.

Jones never had a losing season. He hung banners. He's been a winner his whole life.

We all know who the head coach of this team is going to be, but Jones is in the running to be his one assistant on the All-Time All-Stars. Now the only question is, can he beat out his former teammate?

TOMMY HEINSOHN

Let's get this out of the way first: The absolute best thing about coach Tommy Heinsohn was the suits.

It was the 1970s. There's not much more that needs to be said there. It's just jarring how much they loved plaid back then.

The thing about those suits is they matched Heinsohn's colorful personality. He's always been loud, gruff, and demonstrative. The Heinsohn we see on Celtics broadcasts is only a slight caricature of his usual self.

We already know about Heinsohn's path because he just barely missed being on this team as a player. The one-time Holy Cross standout was a territorial pick for the Celtics in the same draft as K. C. Jones and Bill Russell. He won eight rings as a player, and four years after his playing days were over, he embarked on a coaching career that got him two more.

It didn't start particularly well for him, though. The Celtics suffered their first losing season in 20 years in Heinsohn's first year as coach. Boston was in a transition phase and it showed. Bill Russell had retired and the cupboard of talent was bare.

Then the Celtics drafted Dave Cowens, another near miss for this All-Time All-Star team. Cowens, as you know, was a tough 6'9" big man who Heinsohn installed at center. Heinsohn was going small before anyone thought to go small.

"What he did as a coach—and he coached teams that sometimes were traditional, sometimes weren't— and really had great success," Brad Stevens told ESPN as Heinsohn prepared to be enshrined into the Hall of Fame as a coach.

He had 6'5" and 6'6" Don Nelson and Don Chaney as forwards. Jo Jo White (6'3") and John Havlicek (6'5") were his backcourt. The 6'9" Cowens patrolled the middle.

If this was a video, "I Ran" by A Flock Of Seagulls would start to fade in here, because that's how the Celtics would win games. They ran, and ran, and ran. They were death by a thousand paper cuts, never overwhelming opponents with power, but wearing them to the ground by peppering them with shots over, and over, and over again.

"We made teams crack in these playoffs," Heinsohn once told the *Boston Globe*. "We got them to points in big games in the fourth quarter where they just didn't want to play anymore."

Heinsohn had some freak athletes on his team. Havlicek could run all day because he literally was built to do so by genetic abnormality. Cowens was insanely driven, as were most of his Celtics. But he also drove them to squeeze out every ounce of ability.

"You can bet that you will be ready to go because he made sure we were ready to go," Jo Jo White once said. "He actually shocked me. I was in awe. Because every timeout, every game, every practice, Tommy was right on top of us to make sure we got the job done."

They did that, and then some.

Heinsohn's 1972-73 team still holds the Celtics record for most wins in a season. They went 68-14, but were upset by the eventual champion New York Knicks (he can thank a hard screen by Dave DeBusschere on John Havlicek that debilitated Hondo and effectively forced him to use his left hand throughout the series for that). This was Cowens's MVP season in which he averaged 20.5 points and 16.2 rebounds per game. Heinsohn won Coach of the Year.

They got to the Conference Finals six straight years and won the NBA title twice. The second championship included the triple overtime Game 5 against the Phoenix Suns. By now you've read about all of the superhuman performances in the game.

White played 60 minutes. Havlicek played 58. Cowens 55. However the game might have turned when Heinsohn turned to Glenn McDonald, a barely used second-year player, to replace Paul Silas, who had fouled out.

"I saw Paul fouling out of the game and I was expecting [backup forward Steve] Kuberski to go in and play power forward," McDonald once told Boston.com. "But Tommy goes, 'Mac!' And I just jump up, because maybe he's making a mistake and I'm running in, I want to get in there before he realizes it. But all he said was, 'Run 'em.' Because I had been resting for a while."

He came in and scored six quick points in just about a minute during the third overtime, hitting the game-clinching free throws. Heinsohn turned to a fresh player, even though it was one who didn't play much, to finish off a weary team, and it worked. The Celtics won Game 6.

It all came to an end for Heinsohn soon after that. He clashed with owner Irv Levin, whom Heinsohn has repeatedly called a bad owner. After conflicts and controversial personnel decisions, the Celtics fell into disarray. Heinsohn was fired in 1978 as the Celtics were suffering through an 11-23 start to the season.

"The beauty of coaching the Celtics at the time was that Red Auerbach was in control of the operation, and he kept the owners away," Heinsohn said before his Hall of Fame induction. "So if you were the coach of the team, you could go coach the team and you didn't have to look behind you to see who was knifing you in the back. All the politics of pro basketball was taken away because of Red's ability to do his job. When that evaporated with an owner, and everybody was looking at everybody else with quizzical eyes, it became the worst year-and-a-half of my life. The man that ultimately owned the team, he was trying to coach the team."

Heinsohn went into broadcasting soon after his coaching career ended, and has become a fixture for a new generation of fans.

When we think of the Boston Celtics, we might think of Larry Bird, Bill Russell, or Red Auerbach. Younger people might think of Paul Pierce. But there is only one person on this planet who has been here for almost all of it.

The BAA's Boston Celtics were born in 1946. Heinsohn was drafted 10 years later.

He played until 1965. He immediately joined the Celtics radio broadcast (when he wasn't selling insurance) and did that for three years until he became the coach. He did that until 1978. In 1981 he joined the television broadcast team and has been there ever since.

So as of 2020, the Celtics have existed for 73 years. Heinsohn has been part of the team, somehow, for 60 of them.

Heinsohn is the Boston Celtics. I wouldn't be shocked if he actually bleeds green at this point.

"Tommy was the absolute best," Rivers once told ESPN. "Tommy was great, obviously, when we were winning, but, for me, Tommy was the best when we were losing—those two or three years. He would see me sometimes and just come over and sit with me on the plane. He got it. He just kept telling me over and over, 'You're a really good coach. You're really good. You just need to hang in there.'. . . I don't know how many times he told me that.

"And so when we started winning, it was really cool. The thing I still remember, when we won the title [in 2008], I looked over and Tommy was crying. And I was thinking: He's the true definition of what a Celtic is. And he's the best. Tommy means the world to me."

And he means the world to us.

With all due respect to K. C. Jones, who is Heinsohn's former teammate and a man who also gave a significant portion of himself to the team, the choice here has to be Heinsohn.

He is an innovator. He did small-ball while the NBA forest was still full of redwoods. He is a Hall of Fame coach and one of only five people in the Hall as both a player and a coach. It's only fitting that he makes this All-Time All-Star team as both as well.

So I'm giving him a seat next to Red Auerbach on this coaching bench. If nothing else, they can torture each other like the good ol' days and Tommy can figure out how much of a pain in the ass he was to coach.

Welcome aboard, Tommy.

RED AUERBACH

"Nobody can write a story about the Celtics and not talk about Red Auerbach."

Bill Russell said this in his retirement announcement.

I'm writing a story about the Celtics. So let's talk about Red Auerbach.

Arnold Jacob Auerbach was born in Brooklyn. It's an important thing to note because it may seem to many that he sprung to life magically through the Celtics logo one night. In fact, Auerbach might not have been a Celtic at all had he not had certain moral values.

Red got his nickname like most people get the nickname "Red." He was a fiery red-headed kid who took nothing from anyone. That attitude served him well on the court, where he was a pretty good basketball player. He got a scholarship to George Washington, and as soon as he graduated in 1941, he got into coaching at a local high school.

He joined the Navy and coached their basketball team for three years before being hired to coach the Washington Capitols of the new Basketball Association of America. He immediately led them to the best record in the league in the league's first year, but they were beaten in the semifinals of the playoffs. They missed the playoffs in his second year but returned in the third, losing to the Minneapolis Lakers in the Finals.

Auerbach resigned after a dispute over how to rebuild his team and joined the Duke Blue Devils as an assistant coach. Head coach Gerry Gerard had been diagnosed with cancer, and Auerbach had been promised the head coaching job, but Auerbach quit before that could happen.

Red Auerbach and his trademark cigar in the house that Red built. Today the Celtics floor bears his signature, and the Red Auerbach award is given annually to the Celtics player or coach who best exemplifies the spirit of what it means to be a Celtic through exceptional performance on and off the court. (STEVE LIPOFSKY WWW.BASKETBALLPHOTO.COM)

"I was there until the middle of December and felt funny waiting for him to die," Auerbach said. "So I left Duke and went to Tri-Cities."

Let's just pause to think about what could have happened had Auerbach decided to stay at Duke. Instead of Duke playing at Cameron Indoor Stadium, they could be playing at the Auerbach Center (which is now the name of the Boston Celtics practice facility). The entire course of basketball history changed with Auerbach's decision.

His time at Tri-Cities was short lived. He quit that job too after a conflict over how the team was constructed.

Available once again, Auerbach was put on the radar of Boston Celtics owner Walter Brown by the local media. Brown and Auerbach hit it off. Auerbach, who by this point had quit multiple jobs over disputes with ownership, was pleased with the quality of Brown's character and reputation.

"Walter Brown was a man with no prejudices," Auerbach said. "When he was in the Garden as president and owner of the Celtics, the women that swept the Garden, he would tip his hat to them and open the door for them. There was no such thing as religious or racial prejudice in his own makeup."

This appealed to Auerbach who would play with children of all races and religions in Williamsburg, Brooklyn as a child. When it came time for Auerbach to go through his first draft in 1950, he told Brown the best player to pick was Chuck Cooper, a Black player out of Duquesne.

"I don't care if he's green," Brown said, according to Auerbach. "If he could play, draft him."

And with that Red Auerbach made the selection that broke the NBA's color barrier.

Eventually the Celtics would add Cousy, as you know, despite Auerbach's objections. Once that relationship was ironed out, Auerbach had a point guard that could help lead his vaunted fast-break style of play. Cousy, Bill Sharman, Ed Macauley, and Frank Ramsey would win a high-percentage of regular-season games, but they built a reputation for fading in the playoffs.

After six years of struggling, Bill Russell showed up. It was 1956, and Russell didn't know much about Auerbach as a coach. He also didn't care. He'd had adversarial relationships with coaches his whole life, from the University of San Francisco to the US Olympic team. It's all he knew, and it's all he expected. So when he got to Boston, he was already prepared for that to continue.

"I was completely comfortable with that," Russell wrote in his book, *Red and Me: My Coach, My Lifelong Friend.* "But when I arrived in Boston after the Olympics, Red was secure within himself and I was secure within myself. So he didn't have to prove that he was a great coach, and I didn't have to prove that I was a great player."

It didn't take long for Russell to understand that while they came from different backgrounds, they had a common goal as professionals. He quickly realized that winning trumped all else for Auerbach, just as it did for him.

As they grew over the years, and the two got to know each other better, Russell learned he and Red shared more than basketball philosophies. They had similar philosophical opinions on life.

"We never had to talk about who we were or how to conduct ourselves. We just lived it," he wrote. "Over the next thirteen years, basketball set the stage for our relationship to evolve from caution, to admiration, to trust and respect, to a friendship that lasted a lifetime."

Their partnership spawned nine championships in 10 years, including eight in a row.

Russell was exactly what Red and the Celtics needed. The Celtics were a run-and-gun team, which is where Heinsohn fell in love with the style, but they needed a monster to stop opponents and the Celtics moving the other way. That's why they drafted Russell in the first place.

You don't just give up the Ice Capades without a plan, right?

On Day One, Auerbach made it clear to Russell that he didn't give a damn about his new center shooting the ball.

"He told me right out that he didn't care if I never scored a point," Russell wrote. "He said they had the guys on the Celtics who could score. What he wanted from me was defense and rebounding. That suited me fine."

Part of coaching is understanding who your team is, what the personnel does well, and maximizing it. Auerbach's selection of Russell put both men in a position to do what they do best and excel at the highest levels. He built a juggernaut that he dared the league to challenge.

"Red never scouted that much, because he said, 'I don't give a care what they're going to do; I know what we're going to do,'" Russell said. "That's imposing your will on the game and deciding the pace of the game and how the game's going to be played."

The fast break became a trademark of those legendary Celtics teams. Boston would run teams into the ground, and Auerbach made sure his guys were prepared to do so.

On the first day of training camp, he had his guys press. They played full-court man-to-man the entire day. That probably wouldn't fly today, but back then Auerbach knew that his best chance of winning was with thoroughbreds, so he tested them to see who could handle the workload.

"He wanted a team that was in superior shape," said former Celtic Larry Siegfried. "He didn't have to worry about the team concept stuff, because most of the players that he had up there had come from championship college teams. They had the talent and knew how to win."

The strategy was executed well enough to win 795 games with the Celtics, by far the franchise leader in a record that will be tough to break. After many of those, Red celebrated with his trademark victory cigar.

He once said he detested coaches who continued to pace and gesture when the game was in hand. He accused those coaches, especially the college coaches, of doing so just because they were on TV. To Red, the game was over, and there was no point. A late 25-point lead meant the mission was accomplished, so it was time to move on to the next game.

"So I would light a cigar and sit on the bench and just watch it," Auerbach once, appropriately, told *Cigar Aficionado* magazine. "The game was over, for all intents and purposes. I didn't want to rub anything in or show anybody what a great coach I was when I was 25 points ahead. Why? I gotta win by 30? What the hell difference does it make?

"The commissioner [Maurice Podoloff] said you can't smoke the cigars on the bench. But there were guys smoking cigarettes on the bench. I said, 'What is this, an airplane—you can smoke cigarettes but not cigars?' No way. I wouldn't do it."

Red quit lighting up the sideline cigars in 1966. He turned the team over to his game changer, Bill Russell.

"He and I had one big thing in common—the will to win," Russell wrote. "When he appointed me coach he just said 'The job is yours.' He never put pressure on me. He never even came to practice unless I invited him. Of course, I did—often. I would have been crazy not to take advantage of one of the smartest guys the game has seen."

Red was tough, but he wasn't mean. He demanded a lot, but he didn't demean in the process. He wanted to build something players enjoyed, not feared.

He built Celtics Pride.

NBA history is full of players who don't get it until they get to Boston. It still happens to this day. But what Red built, from the floor to the banners to the sheer mystique, still permeates the franchise.

"Well, I think when people talk about the Celtics mystique, I always think about Red Auerbach," said Nate "Tiny" Archibald, who came to Boston on the downside of his career and won a title.

"As a man behind the scenes, orchestrating everything in those days and building us into a winner, I sincerely thank him for bringing me here. Because I was on the downside or the closing of my career and he revitalized me and gave me a chance to win a championship."

In an interview with the *Harvard Business Review*, Auerbach said, "There's a family feeling. Two people in particular evidenced it for me. One was Wayne Embry, who played at Cincinnati for nine years and came here to finish his career. He never talks about Cincinnati. He talks about Celtics pride and the Celtics organization.

"The other was Paul Silas. One of the best compliments I ever got was from Paul Silas. One day he came over to me and said, 'I heard a lot about this Celtics pride and I thought it was a bunch of crap'—because he was an old veteran when he came here. 'But,' he said, 'I was wrong. I feel a part of it and this has been the happiest part of my career.' It was super. When you hear it from the players, it really makes you feel nine feet tall."

Auerbach had certain luxuries that no longer exist. He played tricks and mind games, for sure. He's also one of, if not the greatest basketball coach, in NBA history. Never mind that he ran the franchise, made draft picks, and executed trades.

Red Auerbach, the cigar-chomping genius motivator of men, sat on those sidelines and created everything this franchise is about. He is, and forever will be, the patriarch of the Boston Celtics.

Final Verdict:
Head Coach: Red Auerbach
Assistant Coach: Tommy Heinsohn

THE GUYS I WISH I COULD VOTE FOR

If I'm going to do this right, I need to make this a little like a real All-Star voting.

Every year, fans get together to vote the best of the best into the All-Star Game while also throwing a few votes to some ... let's call them less-deserving players. A radio team once decided it would be funny to get Zaza Pachulia into the game. Once voting was open to international fans, China would crush the ballot box for not only the deserving Yao Ming, but also undeserving Rockets teammates. Boston Celtics fans in 2020 used their votes to push the 7'6" Tacko Fall into the middle of the pack of the frontcourt voting.

Weird votes are a tradition in NBA All-Star voting. I am a big believer in carrying on tradition.

Also, I just spent a long time thinking very hard about giving the right guys their due. This is my chance to have some fun with the voting. Some of these guys have no business getting votes. Some just deserve a little attention.

Here are guys, in no particular order, I wish I could vote for on the All-Time All-Star team.

Togo Palazzi

First of all, this is an all-time name. Togo played nearly three seasons for the Celtics between 1954 and 1957. He averaged five points and three rebounds over this time, but I was always going to find a way to get Togo Palazzi in this book, and it's not just because of his name.

When I was young, I went to the Providence College basketball camps over the summer to learn and improve my game. After I graduated high school, I'd go back to the PC camps to coach, and some of the coaches from that camp also started a separate camp at Smithfield High School in Smithfield, Rhode Island.

Togo's son Matt, who played at Providence, was involved in both. He brought his dad in to talk to the campers. He talked about playing in the post, and his advice, to the best of my recollection, was, "before a game eat a bunch of garlic. When you get in the post, you turn and you . . ." and he made a big, exaggerated *haaaaaa* exhale sound. "Right in his face. He won't want to guard you after that."

It might be the funniest organic moment I've ever seen. To this day, I wonder if any of those kids took his advice. I picture some impressionable 12-year-old asking mom if they had any garlic in the house, her puzzled look as she asked why, and her reaction when she was told the answer. I wonder if some JV coach walked into a locker room wondering which of his kids doused himself in vampire repellent.

I don't want to know the answer. I just want to believe it happened. I also needed to make sure this story was written down somewhere. This story belongs to the universe because everyone needs to know about that wonderful, wild man named Togo Palazzi.

CHUCK COOPER

I wanted to start on a fun note with Togo, but this is a vote that needs to be in this book somehow.

A story of the history of the Boston Celtics can't be told without Cooper.

He was drafted in the second round of the 1950 NBA Draft, the first draft after the BAA/NBL merger. He was the fourth overall pick, and the first Black player drafted by an NBA team.

Cooper broke pro basketball's color barrier, but it's a distinction he shares with two others.

Cooper was the first to be drafted. Nathaniel "Sweetwater" Clifton was the first to sign a contract (with the New York Knicks). Earl Lloyd was the first Black player to actually play in an NBA game.

Because he was part of a trio of history makers, Cooper didn't quite see his arrival in the NBA as monumental. He actually called it "dubious."

"I wasn't alone," he said, as noted in his *New York Times* obituary. "I didn't have to take the race-baiting and the heat all on my own shoulders like Jackie Robinson. Besides, any black coming after Jackie, in any sport, had it easy compared to the turmoil he lived through."

Easy compared to the turmoil he lived through.

Just because some people were getting used to the idea of Black athletes didn't mean Cooper or any other had it easy in the 1950s.

"It was tough, especially when they traveled down south," Cooper's son told ESPN. "There was one of those times in North Carolina, when my dad couldn't stay at the hotel with the team and he decided to take a train back to Boston. His good friend and his roommate, Bob Cousy, decided to take that train with him."

His Celtics teammates embraced him, even when the rest of the world didn't.

"When Chuck Cooper joined us, some of the players came to me and said this is a little unusual, but we'd like to room with him," Auerbach once said. So I changed roommates every three or four weeks. He roomed with Bones McKinney, who was from the South. He roomed with Cousy, he roomed with Sharman."

The Celtics never had any internal problems with Cooper and his teammates, but despite the comfort the Celtics gave him, Cooper never felt that he could truly grow. Whether it was with Boston, St. Louis, or Fort Wayne, Cooper felt the game didn't want Black stars, and they specifically pushed him into more supporting roles. Cooper didn't shoot or score like he did when he averaged 16 points per game at Duquesne.

"No black superstars were permitted in basketball then," Cooper said. "White management couldn't afford it because they knew white spectators wouldn't put up with it. You sort of had to fit in, if you were going to get in, make your contributions in a subordinate role."

Auerbach vehemently denied such things, at least with the Celtics. Red's entire existence with the Celtics was based on Walter Brown's decency, and he countered that Cooper was just good at rebounding and defense.

It's tough to know exactly where the truth lies. Cooper only shot 34 percent as a pro, but it's hard to imagine playing with a mind free and clear enough to shoot well, even if the outward racism was more tempered than it was in other sports.

Lloyd explained to NPR one important distinction in integrating basketball. Racists, you see, aren't often ones to say things directly to someone's face if there's a threat of repercussion. Racism is cowardly by nature, so any possibility that the target might have something to say or do about it tends to discourage the outward attacks. This is especially true if the target is 6'5" and 200–220 pounds like Cooper and Lloyd.

"Jackie made things a lot easier for me," Lloyd said. "But what happened, if you think about it, Jackie Robinson played first base. The guy playing left field, he can call him all the names he wants to call him and their paths will never cross. But in pro basketball, you stand on a foul line and some guy who might want to call you a name is less apt to—because the proximity is kind of immediate. And there's a little danger involved in calling a guy a name who's standing right next to you."

Cooper died at the age of 57. In an interview with *Pittsburgh* magazine seven years earlier, Cooper said, "people say I look pretty good for 50, but all the damage done to me is inside. That's where it hurts."

Cooper finally made the Naismith Basketball Hall of Fame in 2019, 35 years after his passing. It was a long overdue honor for a man long overdue for proper recognition. His time in the NBA didn't afford him the longevity to make a case for inclusion on this team. Whether his production was race-related, ability-related, or a mix of both, he didn't put up any remarkable statistics.

What he did was put up with a remarkable amount more than anyone should, and he carried a burden with him because of it. He helped open the door in the NBA that changed the league.

BAILEY HOWELL

There are only three viable candidates for power forward in Boston Celtics history, but Howell's four-year run as a Celtic needs to be acknowledged somehow.

Red Auerbach is known for his heists, but the Howell trade is never one that comes up. He took advantage of the Baltimore Bullets glut of power forwards and lack of centers to move seldom-used Mel Counts in return for Howell. Counts played one season for Baltimore, averaging about six points and six rebounds.

Howell was an All-Star in his first season in Boston, averaging 20 points and 8.4 rebounds alongside Bill Russell. He'd average 18 points and 8.4 rebounds over his four-year run in Boston, winning two titles along the way for Russell, who at that point was player-coach.

He didn't have the longevity to legitimately challenge for any of these spots, but it wouldn't be fair to forget Howell's contributions to two championships, or his involvement in one of Auerbach's many lopsided trades.

ANTOINE WALKER

"Why do you take so many 3s?" Walker was once asked.

"Because there are no 4s."

And so begins the story of Antoine Walker in Boston. You've probably heard that quote a bunch, probably because it's an awesome quote.

Antoine Walker came to Boston after two years in Kentucky and immediately made an impact. I almost . . . almost . . . considered him at power forward. That I instinctively didn't is a little telling about his career.

Antoine Walker was known for a signature shimmy, the "Walker Wiggle,"
after he made a big basket. It went along perfectly with his unabashed
shooting from deep. (STEVE LIPOFSKY WWW.BASKETBALLPHOTO.COM)

Part of the problem was when he played. He played during the Rick Pitino years and those are years that folks in Boston want to repress.

Actually his first year was the M. L. Carr year when Boston tried to tank for Tim Duncan. They ended up with Paul Pierce, which ended up working out well. Obviously Duncan worked out better for the Spurs, but, whatever. We're talking about 'Toine here.

"My rookie season was rough as far as wins and losses, but individually I thought I played great from start to finish," Walker said.

He credits Carr for his early success. Even as the Celtics were losing, Walker said Carr provided necessary guidance on and off the court, even calling him a father figure for personal matters.

"He made sure that I did the right things, that I made the right decisions," Walker said. "He helped me with the whole process of transitioning to the NBA because I came into the league at 19 years old and didn't know anything. He really helped me to stay balanced."

Walker made the All-Rookie team. He was a fan-favorite in Boston. He busted out the "Walker Wiggle" after making a particularly impressive shot, or if he got hot from 3. He had a wild knack for making buzzer-beating shots that went in despite having no business actually going in.

The team wasn't great but Antoine's antics were, even though they were also infuriating at the same time.

Let's be clear here: Walker liked to shoot the ball. A lot.

We currently live in the 3-ball era. Guys are encouraged to shoot those shots a lot, but Walker beat them to the race.

Isaiah Thomas, in his 2016-17 season, shot 646 3-pointers, beating Walker's record by one. Walker shot more than 600 3s twice in his career. He almost did it a third time. He's still second all-time in 3-pointers attempted for the Celtics.

If there's any single defining characteristic of Walker's career, it's that he was an unabashed, unrelenting, unapologetic, gunner. It was the single-most dominant topic in any discussion about Walker and his game. It was the subject of many columns and a talking point on just about every radio show discussion about Walker and the Celtics.

At this point in Celtics history, Bill Russell had softened on Boston and seeing him around the team was getting more common. According to Walter McCarty, Russell showed up one day with one of those articles. He showed up in the locker room one day and held it up and said to the players, "The secret's out, that Antoine is going to be taking a ton of shots, and that if we wanted to get our shots we shouldn't wait for him to pass—we should wait for him to miss."

Sick burn, right? Then it gets better, because he looked Walker straight in the face and added, "From what I've seen out of your shot selection, there should be plenty of misses to go around."

You'd think having one of the greatest players the NBA has ever seen come into a locker room to bust your balls would be a wake-up call. Instead, he took even more.

Once Pitino was dispatched and Jim O'Brien took over, Walker doubled how many 3-pointers he took, jumping from 3.5 per game to 7.4 in the 2001 season. He averaged just under eight 3-pointers per game over his final three seasons as a Celtic in O'Brien's "let it fly" style.

As an aside, I bumped into O'Brien in an airport in 2019 as we were each traveling to our next NBA city. I asked him how many 3s Walker would have taken in today's NBA and his reaction was a combination of a laugh and an eye-roll. I forget what he said, exactly, but the tone of his answer was basically that if you thought he was a gunner before, he'd blow your mind today.

Shot happy or not, Walker did have some success in Boston, averaging 20.6 points and 8.7 rebounds per game in eight seasons as a Celtic. He made three All-Star teams. He got a shoe commercial!

Walker was also part of the most amazing playoff comeback in NBA history.

On May 25, 2002, Walker, Pierce, and the sixth-seed Celtics were down 74–53 heading into the fourth quarter against the top-seed New Jersey Nets. They'd already shocked the Philadelphia 76ers. (Remember Allen Iverson's rant about practice? It came during this series.) They took out the second-seeded Pistons, and now they were tied 1–1 with the Nets, but down 21 to start the final quarter.

Paul Pierce scored 19 points in that quarter. Walker had six rebounds and an assist. Boston outscored the Nets 41–16 and won the game by four. Walker calls it the highlight of his career.

"It was probably my finest moment in a Boston Celtics uniform. Being able to win that game, and going up 2–1 in that series, and believing that we could actually get this team to the Finals," he said. "An incredible moment in my career. Whenever I'm in Boston, people still bring it up."

The Celtics lost that series, as they should have, but that win will live forever in Celtics history. Walker was definitely a big part of Boston's story, but not big enough for me to consider him among the All-Stars. He shot 41 percent, and I can't excuse it away due to the era. He was the classic volume scorer who could only get his true shooting percentage over .500 once. Sadly what he's most known for nowadays is his blown fortune. Walker is a classic cautionary tale of excess in pro sports. Between the lavish lifestyle and caring for hangers-on, all of his NBA money is gone.

He has since worked as a consultant who helps other players avoid making the same mistakes.

WALTER MCCARTY

Walker's Kentucky and Celtics teammates can thank Tommy Heinsohn for this mention, because it was his "*I love Waltah*" exultations that made McCarty a household name.

Heinsohn loved McCarty's ability to do all the little things no one wanted to do. McCarty wasn't going to make it in the NBA by scoring a ton of points. He had to fill in the gaps in games and make what's known as the 50-50 plays, the plays where each guy has an equal chance at the ball, to get on the floor. Heinsohn appreciated that in McCarty, maybe more than anyone.

McCarty described his role as "play great defense, shut down the other team's best scorer, run the floor, knock down shots in the flow of the offense, and hustle all over the court. I was the guy who scrapped for the rebound, who would dive on the floor for loose balls—you know, the type of player who did a lot of the dirty work that maybe other players didn't like to do."

Fans can thank McCarty's hustle and dirty work for the creation of a new sort of metric, the Tommy Point, born from

In one game broadcast, Tommy Heinsohn spoke directly to McCarty as he was checking in, imploring him to run and play the up-tempo ball Heinsohn loved and that the Celtics team needed in order to succeed. (STEVE LIPOFSKY WWW.BASKETBALLPHOTO.COM)

the brain of Heinsohn and meant to honor guys like McCarty who didn't rack up traditional stats.

While most people focused on the big scorers and rebounders, Heinsohn wanted to be sure someone who did the little things like McCarty got recognition too. If it wasn't for McCarty being the type of guy to do all that, we might not have the "Tommy Point." They've become a huge part of Celtics broadcasts. Every time someone would dive for a ball, rip a rebound away from an opponent, or just do something out of sheer hustle and will, Heinsohn would scream "*That's a Tommy point!*"

It didn't take long for fans to show up to games with signs asking for Tommy Points. It became part of the Celtics culture.

Heinsohn has backed off from doing the games full-time, but the Tommy Award was created for every broadcast to give a player special recognition of a job well done, even if his statistics didn't jump off the page.

JIM LOSCUTOFF

Dave Cowens's number 18 hangs from the rafter, but it only does because the original number 18, Jim Loscutoff, let it happen.

Loscutoff needs a mention simply in case fans don't know he's the "LOSCY" who hangs along with the retired numbers.

You see, back in the '60s the Celtics were quick to retire the numbers of career Celtics who helped win championships, and Loscutoff was one of them. He played nine seasons with Boston and helped them win their first title. He was part of seven championship teams overall, and served mostly as one of the team's enforcers.

"He was cantankerous and didn't back down from anyone, Wilt (Chamberlain) included," his former teammate Ernie Barrett once said. "So nobody pushed him around on the court [laughs]. And he could run. He never stopped running."

His best season was a 10.6-point, 10-3-rebound double-double year he averaged in 1957, the year Boston finally broke through and won a title. He was a poor shooter, though, even for his time. Still, Auerbach built the Celtics on the concept of family and loyalty and to him that meant rewarding Loscutoff by retiring his number 18.

Loscy, as he was known, refused. He told Auerbach he didn't want to deprive anyone else from wearing the number. So Red, being stubborn, wanted to retire something in his honor, so he retired the nickname.

Don Nelson

In 2019, Nelson was asked about his post-retirement life during a news conference. He calmly grabbed the microphone and said . . .

"I've been smoking some pot."

And that's Nellie. He'd graduated from beers, probably to the benefit of his liver, to marijuana. As a coach, he was once told by the league he couldn't bring beers to the podium after games.

How can I not want to vote for this guy?

He signed with Boston in 1965 and ultimately became a legend as one of the game's greatest sixth men.

The one thing that always stood out about Nelson was his jump shot. Nelson's soft touch was honed on an Iowa farm out of necessity. Missed shots would often find their way into piles

Nelson's playing days were overshadowed by his coaching days, when "Nellie Ball" was a run-and-gun extension of the fast-break style taught by Red Auerbach and Tommy Heinsohn. He entered the Hall of Fame as a coach, and is the only coach with more than 1,000 wins as a coach and multiple championships as a player. (WIKIMEDIA COMMONS)

of chicken waste, so he made sure to get arc on his shot and not miss long.

In fact that soft shot helped secure one of the five championships won during Nellie's time in Boston.

With the Celtics up one in Game 7 in Los Angeles, the ball was tipped away from John Havlicek and it kicked over to Nelson at the free throw line. Nellie picked up and calmly fired a feathery jumper that kicked off the back of the rim, straight up into the air, and down through the net to beat the shot clock.

This is the game more famously known as "the balloon game," the one I wrote about in the Bill Russell section. Nelson had 16 points in that Game 7. His jumper was the killer for the Lakers, and it gave Russell his eleventh ring in his final season.

Russell made a promise, and Nellie helped him keep it. He sent Russell out a winner, so I repeat, how can I not vote for this guy?

Nellie got to go out on top too, winning a title in 1976 and calling it a career. With five rings and remarkable consistency off the bench, Auerbach honored Nelson by retiring his number 19 in 1978.

You might know Nellie better for taking Red's run-and-gun style and turning it into a Hall of Fame coaching career. "Nellie Ball," much like Heinsohn's fast-break style, all came from the Auerbach coaching tree.

Nellie, you've had a hell of a run. You can enjoy some trees of another kind on your estate in Hawaii. Me? I'm gonna crush a brew and toast you like the good ol' days.

CHUCK CONNORS

If you're old enough to remember the TV show *The Rifleman*, then you know Chuck Connors. What some of you don't know is that he not only played for the Celtics, but was one of about a dozen guys who played in both Major League Baseball and the NBA.

I just think that's cool.

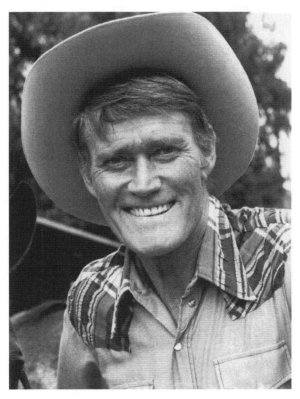

In a weird twist, two players named Chuck can claim "The Rifleman." Connors, who starred in the series, and later Indiana Pacers wing Chuck Person, who claimed the nickname for his shooting prowess. (NBC TELEVISION VIA WIKIMEDIA COMMONS)

EVAN TURNER

Turner might be the most quotable player of all time. Here are a selection of quotes for you to enjoy, and then you try to tell me afterwards how I can't give this guy a vote. This selection comes from a Reddit thread called "The Evan Turner quote master list." Please note, his quotes are so amazing, someone created a Reddit thread to make sure they didn't miss any. After you put this book down, I'd suggest you go search that on Reddit. You can thank me later.

On a return to Philadelphia, where he was originally drafted:
"Before the game I signed like 100,000 autographs, I'm kissing babies and what not and all that stuff. I'm getting my hand kissed by people; I got little girls come up to me, fainting. Once the game started, it was like, 'What the hell is going on?' I was like, 'This is weird. Did they take all the good people out?' . . . I don't worry about it anymore. I don't want to sound super weird, but Jesus was hated, too. At the end of the day, I just worry about the stuff that's important. If it makes you happy to boo me, go ahead. I'm still happy. I put all that stuff behind me."

On passing to Jae Crowder for a game-winning shot in 2015:
"When I was dribbling, I was like, 'Oh, snap, I'm at 15 feet, I'm about to end this.' And then I thought about [Michael Jordan] passing to Steve Kerr. And I thought, 'Well, let me add that to my legacy. I'll pass one time.' And that was it. It was unbelievable, actually. Ingenious by me."

On being told he's coming off the bench:
"[Brad Stevens] spoke to me. I had to smell his breath for alcohol. I checked his office for drugs. I said, 'You've gotta be high.' You know what I'm saying? But I kept it classy, of course,

and I trust the process. And that was it. But it's unbelievable, right?"

And most recently, in a return to Boston, on Marcus Smart becoming known for wearing robes:

"I don't know if you know who used to do the robes all the time. Y'all know who did the robes? . . . Go ask my man Andy Mannix and he'll tell you who used to pull up with the robes all the time. Go ask my man JJ how I got the name Hugh Hefner. You know what I'm saying? Smart's robes are nicer than mine. I just use the local hotel robes and I see that Versace looks like it's pretty nice. Not to go talk to kids in the robe, I learned that. I definitely dig the steez. I definitely dig the steez. Marcus Smart is a great teammate and a great memory for me."

When he was asked a follow-up of whether he was a silk robe or towel robe kind of guy, he said:

"Depends. If I'm fresh out the shower, I'm a towel. I gotta dry off. Then every now and then, when 8 p.m. hits, I have a guest over. A little red wine, put on a little Sade or something, that silk comes out. It's over from there, you feel me?"

Oh we feel you, ET. We feel you.

Turner can never retire. If he does, he just needs to travel the country being interviewed. It's what the world demands.

BILL WALTON

Bill Walton is what happens when you mix Don Nelson and Evan Turner together in a lab.

Walton is a true NBA legend, but he's also a true human legend. He is one of the most skilled big men ever to play the game.

By the time he'd come to Boston, he was almost literally on his last leg. Walton had endured injury after injury in his time in the NBA, sapping him of years of greatness.

Walton calls himself the most injured player ever, and it's hard to dispute. He had a 14-year NBA career, but missed four full seasons due to injury. He had another four seasons where he played less than 35 games and then another three where he played between 51 and 58 games.

"I spent half of my adult life in the hospital, endured 37 operations, and never achieved the ultimate dream of being the best," he said. "I've learned to appreciate the things that I've accomplished, like being a part of two of the greatest basketball teams in the world, the (UCLA) Bruins and the Celtics. It doesn't get much better than that."

This is why I want Walton in. Yeah, he can be a little bit of a space shot.

OK, a lotta bit . . .

But along with the flowery prose he's become known for, there is a deep appreciation for the moments, even when they come in the midst of the worst things he's felt.

For example, he once compared spending time with Larry Bird to being on a tropical island.

"There is so much heat, and so much life, and everything is happening at warp speed," he said. "I don't know if you have ever been to Maui, but you can sit there in a chair and see the plants get bigger because everything is happening at such an extreme level."

He takes you down this acid trippy jaunt of a story, and then he hits you with a dose of positivity at the end. After all that, he says he's the luckiest guy in the world to have experienced that.

Walton missed out on a lot of opportunities to create a greater legacy, but his time with the Celtics allowed him to face some of the NBA's legends, like Michael Jordan and Kareem Abdul-Jabbar, one more time.
(STEVE LIPOFSKY WWW.BASKETBALLPHOTO.COM)

The man took the T, Boston's subway system, to games because he hated sitting in traffic. Just imagine that for a second. You're standing there in Cambridge and a Red Line train pulls up. You step on, and there's seven feet of Bill f'ing Walton sitting there on his way to a game. How does anyone react to something like that?

Walton said he'd be on trains that were rocking with Celtics fans, so that's some sort of answer. His descriptions of playing in the Garden, from the wild fans to the ushers letting people in through a back entrance, are nothing short of amazing. And after each story he tells, he says some version of the same thing: "I'm lucky to have experienced it."

Walton's enduring positivity is heartwarming. It's a joy every time I hear it. So many people focus on where his mind wanders. If you listen until the end, you'll always find it leads to his heart.

THE BOSTON CELTICS
ALL-TIME ALL-STAR TEAM

Head Coach:	Red Auerbach
Assistant Coach:	Tommy Heinsohn
Point Guard:	Bob Cousy
Reserve:	Jo Jo White
Shooting Guard:	John Havlicek
Reserve:	Sam Jones
Small Forward:	Larry Bird
Reserve:	Paul Pierce
Power Forward:	Kevin McHale
Reserve:	Kevin Garnett
Center:	Bill Russell
Reserve:	Robert Parish
Wild Cards:	Dave Cowens, Tommy Heinsohn

SOURCES

Websites

AlanPaul.net
Basketball-reference.com
Boston.com
Celtic-Nation.com
CollegeHoopsDaily.com
ESPN.com
Grantland.com
HuffingtonPost.com
Investors.com
MassLive.com
NBA.com
Reddit.com
RedsArmy.com
SBNation.com
Slamonline.com
SportsMediaNews.com
TheUndefeated.com
TimesReporter.com

News Media Archives
Boston Globe
Boston magazine
CBS Boston
Chicago Tribune
Indy Star
Los Angeles Times
NBC Sports Boston
New York Times
Sports Illustrated
Washington Times

BIBLIOGRAPHY

Cohen, Robert W. *The 40 Greatest Players in Boston Celtics History*. Guilford, CT: Down East Books, 2017.

Reynolds, Bill. *Cousy: His Life, Career, and the Birth of Big-Time Basketball*. New York: Simon & Schuster, 2005.

Taylor, John. *The Rivalry: Bill Russell, Wilt Chamberlain, and the Golden Age of Basketball*. New York: Random House, 2005.

Thomas, Ron. *They Cleared the Lane: The NBA's Black Pioneers*. Lincoln, NE: Bison Books, 2004.

ACKNOWLEDGMENTS

I never thought I'd ever write a book, much less be approached to write one about my true passion in life, basketball and the Boston Celtics. This is much different than anything I've ever written, and there were more than a few times when I said to myself, "What are you even doing here?"

So the first thank you goes out to Niels Aaboe and the entire group at Lyons Press and Rowman & Littlefield who gave me this opportunity and helped guide me through it. The imposter syndrome in me still says I screwed this whole thing up, so if you've gotten this far in the book, it's because they bailed me out.

I never expected to be here. This basketball journey has been full of surprises, and this is just the latest in a long line of them. To properly thank those involved, I have to go back to the beginning of it all.

Thanks to my mother, Artemis, for taking me to my first baseball practice when I was young. If she didn't drag me to that, I don't know that I would have ever gotten into sports at all. I was perfectly happy to be the chubby little kid reading books, but she introduced me to a world of sports that set me on this path.

My high school coach, Roger Berard, didn't have to keep me on the team. I was still chubby and I couldn't do a pushup or make a layup, but I was 6'3" and he said, "You can't coach height," so he set about turning me into a real player. I remember Jacek Duda, then a Providence College player, coming to practice and giving me a hard lesson in playing in the post. I went to PC basketball camps every summer and, by the time I was a senior, I'd become an actual player being recruited by colleges. None of this happens without Coach Berard's faith.

That was a long transformation for me, and my father, despite being a small business owner with ridiculous demands on his time, was always there. One of my favorite photos is a yearbook picture with me in my road blues grabbing a rebound and my father, blurry in the background, sitting in the stands by himself. The sick bastard even came to a college game while having a heart attack, which sounds like something out of an SNL "Bill Swerski's Superfans" sketch, but it really happened. Thanks, Joe, for all the support over the years, and even the tough love from time to time.

College was a turning point in my life. My Emerson College experience was something I didn't expect, but one I'll cherish forever. Hank Smith changed my life by giving me a heavy dose of reality. I grew up more in the two years I spent with him than I ever thought I could. Tough love doesn't even begin to describe it. I didn't realize it when it was happening, but the lessons I was learning with him over those two years were lessons I'd carry with me forever. There were moments where I flat-out hated him, but once I was out of that college bubble, I realized those moments prepared me for some of life's harshest realities. Everything he did was to get me to be my best. I'm happy to say that it worked, Hank. So much of what has allowed me to find success in basketball stems from those lessons . . . even if I had to sift through a steady stream of profanity to find it.

I have to give a special shout-out to Bruce Seals, one of our assistant coaches and a former NBA player. He played for Bill Russell, and he taught me how to deal with a hard-ass coach. Bruce, I only wish I could have learned all those tricks you were trying to teach us when you were trying to teach them. It took me six years to finally get that Euro-step down, but you'll be happy to know that in that moment, at some league in Watertown, I pulled that move off and thought of you.

I was lucky to have some great teammates, and some wild experiences that might fill another book if I ever wanted to sit down and recall them all. I thought about listing all your names but I don't want to embarrass myself and forget someone. Just know that all of you, from nights watching *Stripes* to wild van rides and everything in between, hold a special place in my heart.

To Kate and the boys, I thank you for understanding why I disappeared for so long. Your love and support made this book a reality. The same goes to my brother Nick and my sister Arestea, who thought me moving back to Boston was going to be a chance for all of us to spend more time together but instead it ended up being less.

To Dave, John, Mike, and Victor: Your friendship has carried me through my highest highs and lowest lows. None of this is possible without you guys being there for me at nearly every turn in my life. I love you all like brothers.

And most importantly, I have to thank Del.

Carlos "Del" Broussard and I almost instantly bonded. We met at Emerson when he heard me blasting Big Daddy Kane from two floors away. He taught me the origins of rap music, about hip-hop culture, about the roots in jazz and blues. We were a yin and yang: me, a Celtics fan from Rhode Island, him a Lakers fan from Los Angeles.

My world forever changed the day I learned you were gone. I always knew you needed help, but I never realized just how much. It's been decades, but I still miss you, Del. I always will, and I'll always fight for greater awareness of mental health in your honor, because the best way to remember you and carry on your legacy is to help someone else.

I think of you all the time, Del. Thank you for the time we had, even if it wasn't how much time I wanted.

This is dedicated to you.